MAY I HELP YOU?

An Insight to Better Customer Service
For Black-Owned Businesses

Damon Darrell

Published by Two Trees Publishing Group Po Box 934 Mullica Hill, NJ 08062

Library of Congress Cataloging-in-Publication Data (if applicable)

ISBN: 978-0-9837587-2-3

Cover design by Asif Ali

Interior design by Priya Paulraj

Copyediting by Jessica B. Smith of WriteSmith Productions

Printed in United States of America

For additional copies, bulk purchases, or special sales, please contact Two Trees Publishing Group at sales@twotreespg.com.

Contents

Foreword

"And whatsoever ye do, do *it* heartily, as to the Lord, and not unto men; Knowing that of the Lord ye shall receive the reward of the inheritance: for ye serve the Lord Christ"

— Colossians 3:23-24

I know what you're thinking, oh boy…a bible verse. What's this guy's angle? Well before you toss this book aside, please allow me to share the basis on why this bible verse serves as a fundamental guide for the material presented in this book. Yes, I am Christian. But here is what I am not. I am not an overzealous bible thumper who casts judgment on those who may have different beliefs than I do. However, I am not ashamed nor afraid to share some of the biblical principles that now govern and guide every aspect of my life, including business.

Through my own spiritual journey, I have learned that the fundamental laws of God are applicable in many practical situations. By focusing on pleasing God through our own works and actions, we will undoubtedly elevate the level of service that we provide to our fellow man.

No matter what your belief system is, acknowledging and submitting to a higher authority allows each of us to remain humble, thus allowing us to set ourselves aside and provide the quality level of customer service that our customers deserve. This simple ideology can mean the difference between success and failure. If we are able to elevate ourselves spiritually, then we can reasonably expect to see that same energy translate into successful business practices. I believe that serving God ultimately teaches us to serve each other.

Whether you accept it or not, as a business owner you are a steward over what God has given you, which essentially means that you work for God, who is the true owner of everything. Good customer service, in my humble opinion, begins with us learning to serve God, wholeheartedly, cheerfully, and submissively. Circumventing this process only leads to the self-serving, egotistical pitfalls that have plagued mankind since the beginning of time.

Please keep in mind that while I am writing this book to specifically target issues that black business owners face around customer service, this book is in no way restricted to only people of color. The fact is, I am a black man, who loves all people, but I openly admit that I have an overwhelming desire to specifically see black-owned businesses succeed.

So with the submission of this discourse, I humbly share with you years of experience, examples, and best practices which were cultivated from my own observations and interactions from the rounded perspective of both proprietor and consumer. In these pages, I hope that you find valuable insight and useful tools that will help elevate the level of customer service that you provide to your customers. Enjoy!

CHAPTER 1

My Two Cents

If you are reading this book then at some point you may have experienced a less than stellar customer service interaction with a black-owned business or you are a black-owned business owner and value your customers so much that you are willing to invest some level of effort into improving your customer service situation.

So, what makes me qualified to speak on this touchy subject? The answer is simple. Experience. I have over 20 years of collective customer service experience. On-the-job trainings, countless hours of sigma six coaching, and hundreds of Gallup evaluations. I've gone from working concession stands to holding upper management positions. I've worked in banking, serving high profile business clients and now as a business owner, I have cultivated those experiences into the tools necessary to deliver first-class customer service to my own clients.

Why is this book important? Or rather how will this book help you? That answer is also simple. _How May I Help You?_ is intended to be an unofficial guide to better customer service practices for businesses owned by black entrepreneurs. With all of the recent social uproar and injustices surrounding people of color, there has been a call to action for people of color to make a congenial effort to support more black-owned businesses.

Why is this important? Other than feeling good about supporting our own people and promoting the idea of solidarity, buying black helps extend the circulation period of the dollar within the black community. More and more organizations and institutions are spotlighting the ideology behind economic empowerment. There is a lot of research out there suggesting that money circulates only one time within the black community, opposed to the six to nine times in other non-black communities. There are tons of articles and other resources out there that explore this subject matter in detail, and I urge you to do your own research and educate yourself on the subject. I must warn you—once you start down this rabbit hole, there will be an endless, but enlightening journey ahead of you. Some things you will not be able to unlearn, but all for the greater good.

Today, African American consumers spend approximately $900 billion dollars a year, and it is estimated that by 2030 will wield over $1 trillion dollars of buying power, making us the most highly targeted group for marketers and advertisers. If you are a business owner, specifically a black business owner, I would assume that you are targeting the same group and if you are not, then shame on you.

Once again you may ask, why is this important and what does this have to do with customer service? Well, that answer is a little bit more complicated. Whenever I hear someone suggest that black folk need to support black-owned businesses, I immediately hear a barrage of gripes. To be fair, there are a lot of valid points coming from both sides of the equation; however, I do believe there is a compromise to be had. The truth is that everyone has experienced bad customer service from all kinds of businesses. But why are black businesses singled out and end up taking most of the heat? Stay tuned, because we are about to explore what I think could be part of the problem!

CHAPTER 2

The Black Factor

How many times have you gone into a big box retail store or a big brand restaurant and received poor service? Probably hundreds. What did you think about that experience? If you are being honest, you probably grumbled for a moment or maybe you even posted a bad review online, but more than likely, a week or two later you were back at the same store or restaurant, rolling the dice, hoping that you get better customer service this go-round. Maybe you did and maybe you didn't, but months go by and you become less and less concerned about receiving good customer service. In fact, you begin to expect poor service as a routine function of life.

Why do you do that? To put it simply, we all at some point become creatures of habit and convenience. The fundamental principles of service become benign and without question, we continue to hand over our hard-earned cash to businesses that no longer value us or our patronage. If this is in fact a true assessment of what society has become accustomed to, why is it that when we frequent a black-owned establishment, the expectation for greatness almost triples? Why is it that someone can leave a big brand store and be complacent with subpar service and, in the same day, visit a black-owned establishment and expect impeccable five-star service with no room for error?

I have a theory, and it's called "the black factor". According to Merriam Webster's dictionary, the word "factor" is defined as a quantity by which a given quantity is multiplied or divided in order to indicate a difference in measurement. Let's dive deeper into the word "quantity" within this definition. Again, Merriam Webster's dictionary tells us that quantity means the aspect in which a thing is measurable in terms of greater, less, or equal or of increasing or decreasing magnitude.

Now, if "black" is the thing being measured in terms of increasing magnitude, it only makes sense that "the black factor" is a measurement placed on black-owned businesses that increases in magnitude when it comes to expectation. This is the one ideology that places additional pressure on "black" owned businesses and puts them in a position where they are expected to deliver a much higher level of service without necessarily having the same resources available to them that may be available to non-black-owned businesses and big brand stores.

Yes, I know, it's a lot to digest. African American people are one of the major culprits of adding "the black factor" to their customer service experience when patronizing black-owned establishments. Of course there is an argument to be made that justifies our belief in this practice.

The argument is based on a theory I have developed from my own personal observations, my own personal experiences, and my own investigatory efforts. Whenever I hear the cliché phrase "That's why I don't support black businesses", the critical thinker in me always wonders why? Why is this such a point of contention? Why does this hurt so deep? Why do black-owned businesses get only one chance while other businesses get many? As I attempt to answer this question, I can't help but think that the root of this idealism lies deep within the oppressive construct of a prejudicial society where discrimination is the cornerstone of nearly every institution in this country. What does that mean? It means that African Americans have always had to work harder for less. Of course, one could argue that things have gotten better over the years. One could argue that more and more opportunities are available now and that one can find success in this country if they pull themselves up by the bootstraps. Once again, I have to raise that pesky critical-thinkers flag and ask, how does one pull themselves up by the bootstraps if they don't own boots?

In this country, African Americans have always been behind the proverbial eight ball, making it nearly impossible to accomplish high levels of success consistently. However, being the resilient people that we are, we have reached many levels of success despite the deliberate obstacles placed in our paths. African Americans have always been excluded from the congenialities of this prosperous nation, and because of this, it makes sense for African Americans to be in concert with one another when it comes to business and patronage. It makes sense that this group of people, who have always been marginalized, band together in a unified display of financial solitude. So, when a fellow African American man or woman decides to give a black-owned business their hard-earned money, the expectation is that they receive the highest level of customer service. Not only is it a way to say thank you for your business in a world that roots against your success, it sends a unified message to the world, confirming that the power of the black dollar is strong and capable of sustaining our communities.

I know. Wow right! Something as simple as saying "How may I help you" or "I appreciate your business" can make a meaningful impact on the way black dollars are circulated within the black community. Black-owned businesses cannot afford to neglect "the black factor". It's the one dynamic that connects us and divides us at the same time. The audacity of expectation. When a cruel world gives your customers the cold shoulder, it is your responsibility to embrace your African American customers with an exaggerated level of warmth and compassion, something that they will never get anywhere else.

I truly believe that this is why African American customers take this so personally. They expect to be treated well by their own and when they are not, they feel betrayed, hence, "the black factor" in full effect.

Now it goes without saying that you should treat all of your customers with the utmost dignity and respect. Keep in mind that owning a business comes with great responsibility, a responsibility that transcends personal gratification but instead represents a healthy and cohesive financial infrastructure within the black community.

If we look to history, we will find that African American proprietorship is not a new concept. In fact, many freed and enslaved African Americans operated small businesses. With the end of the Civil War and the issuance of the Emancipation Proclamation, the country was forced to assimilate the newly freed slaves into the framework of America. During this Reconstruction Era, Black Americans began to loosely chase the American Dream. Of course with the realization of political, social, educational, and economic advancements of the black community, many white Americans were enraged at the boldness of black progression. This perpetual hatred of black success gave birth to the era of Jim Crow. Jim Crow laws were created to legalize and enforce racial segregation. The main goal of the Jim Crow movement was to marginalize the newly inducted African American citizen.

White proprietors began to limit or completely cease relationships with black consumers. Because of this, the need for products and services in the black community skyrocketed and soon after, black entrepreneurs began to fill the void. I know…you didn't pick up a copy of this book for a traumatic stroll through history; however, if we are going to address this topic truthfully and wholeheartedly, we must first acknowledge the painful tenant of racism that serves as the backdrop to this story. Some may liken this ideology to the so-called "critical race theory" which scrutinizes how the legacy of slavery and segregation in America is embedded in modern-day legal systems and policies. Some people are threatened by the mere mention of calling foul on such a flagrant play. Perhaps it's because they know that if forced to play the game fairly without an implied advantage, they may find themselves slipping from first place. I simply call the facts the truth. There is no level of negotiation, white washing, or manipulation of facts that will change the truth. Without truth, we have no hope of evolving. Without truth, we have no way of cultivating those principles that will ultimately champion our pathway to those viable business opportunities within our own communities. Without having a true and unobstructed understanding of our past, no matter how disparaging or disheartening, we will never be able to understand those consequential dogmas that contribute to "the black factor". It's a lot—I know. Now might be a good time to grab some coffee or a cup of herbal tea before jumping into the next chapters of potential solutions that can help us navigate our way to better customer service.

CHAPTER 3

Do You Have a Business or a Side Hustle?

Everyone has a different motive for starting a business. Some people are driven by the need or desire of money. Some people will create a business entity purely for tax advantages and some people are just born with that burning desire to live life as an entrepreneur. Here's where it's going to sting a little bit. Some people are not equipped to be business owners. That doesn't make them bad people; it simply suggests that certain individuals may lack the necessary business acumen to run a business successfully.

Picture this. It's the weekend and you have finally carved out time to make those scented candles you have been obsessing about all week. After a few trips to the art store and a few hours of mixing and experimenting while sipping your favorite wine, you develop this masterpiece of pure aromatic bliss. You invite your friends over for drinks and a good time, then suddenly, one of your day ones asks that magical question: "What is that smell?"

You begin to explain how you came into your new hobby and the next thing you know, you're being convinced and cajoled into selling your great smelling wares. As you pursue your newfound passion, you suddenly realize that selling products and providing customer service is actually hard work and requires more time and effort than simply mixing up a batch of those oh so special strawberry-kiwi scented candles that all your friends rave about. Of course, you probably spend eight hours a day at a job you probably hate and at some point, you were actually banking on this side hustle to be lucrative enough to boost you into early retirement.

Three months into it, you realize that you have orders backing up and you're having difficulties finding some of the key ingredients required to make your candle with consistent quality. On top of everything, your boss has given you an extra project that requires you to work overtime. At this point you start to care less and less about the orders and are secretly cursing your bestie for putting this ridiculous idea into your head.

A few more days go by and you decide to search the internet in hopes of locating the materials you need to make your candles and fill those outstanding orders. You find a great online wholesaler that has exactly what you need at a great price so you eagerly begin filling out the order form until... the form requests you to fill in your EIN? Wait! What is an EIN?! No one told you that you needed one of those. Now you cannot complete your order because the wholesale website only does transactions with businesses that have a verifiable EIN number.

In the heat of frustration, you push your laptop to the side and pour yourself a huge glass of wine. Again, you start to care less and less about those orders. After all, your favorite show is on and you are already two episodes behind.

A few more days go by and you notice that your social media is blowing up and not in a good way. Everyone is dragging your name through the mud and wishing impending doom on your yet to be born grandchildren. Or even worse, they are waiting to catch you outside (oh yes, it does get that serious!).

Your first thought is to log into your online store and refund all of the money, but, while going through the process you realize how much money you are about to lose because of the credit card transaction fees that have been deducted. Oh well, you thought. You'll just do your best to fulfill any outstanding orders for now, and then something else hits you. Shipping! Oh no! You forgot to include shipping. Now your profit has taken a dive into the negative because you now realize that you are losing at least $4 per order in shipping alone. So what do you do now?

This is when you have a long discussion with yourself and decide whether you want to abandon ship or continue pursuing this as a full-time business. Of course abandoning ship doesn't mean screwing over your existing customers who have already placed orders; however, there is a way to bow out gracefully. Communicate, apologize, and deliver. Let your customers know that there were a few issues that caused some delays and assure them that their orders will be on the way soon. Remember communicate, don't converse. People don't want to hear your life story. They don't care that you have a full-time job and had to suddenly work loads of unexpected overtime. The only thing they know is that they spent $14.95 on a candle that they have not received yet. Either way, you have earned a spot on the "that's why I don't support black businesses" list.

So let's assume you have decided to stick with it and turn this disastrous attempt of entrepreneurship into a viable business venture. Before you begin, there are a few things that you need to consider before diving in head first. The next chapter discusses the importance of looking the part before living the part. Remember that EIN that we talked about a little while ago? Well, that is only a small piece of the puzzle. There are many things that you will need to know if you want to run a trustworthy business. So grab another cup of coffee, a notebook, and let's dive in!

CHAPTER 4

The Unbalanced Equation

O kay, so now that we have addressed "the black factor", we need to address the rest of the equation. One of the biggest complaints I hear about black-owned businesses are in regards to high prices. I get it. Why would you pay $4.00 for a roll of toilet paper when you can go to the big box store and get it for $1.00? Well, for one thing, it's what we have to do as black consumers. We have to train ourselves to commit to supporting black-owned businesses even if the prices are sometimes slightly higher than big retail stores. Of course, this is executed within reason. We all work hard for a dollar and one has a reasonable argument that spending more when you don't have to is not a financially sound thing to do. However, there are exceptions to the rule (in my humble opinion, of course!)

Black-owned businesses need the support of black consumers. Why? Because they may not receive the support otherwise. I believe it is our responsibility to ensure that black-owned businesses have an equitable chance at survival. Some of you may agree, some may not, but I ask you to consider the following.

Black-owned businesses do not always have access to wholesale price breaks or buying groups that some of the big retailers have access to. Where a big retail store can probably buy a case of toilet paper for pennies on the dollar, most black-owned businesses depend on those retail stores as their wholesale suppliers...at retail prices.

Another major issue that black business owners face is a lack of access to capital. This means they initially don't have an adequate amount of money saved to sustain their business or they do not have the ability to secure financing from a financial institution to fill those budgetary gaps. Why is this such an important factor? If you understand a business's cash flow cycle, then you know that access to funds for inventory is critical to a business's survival. Unfortunately, access to funds needed to buy products and materials is necessary to sustain a business on a **consistent** level. If sales don't come in fast enough, the business owner cannot restock or reinvest in their business. This explains why some businesses may routinely find themselves running out of product. Without access to business loans and lines of credit, business owners are forced to default to the cash and carry method of running their business. They also lack the ability to invest in the necessary equipment needed to sustain the basic infrastructure of their business.

A business loan allows you to do things like make renovations to a store plan, thereby making browsing easier for your customers as they peruse your merchandise. It may also mean purchasing new equipment to help your business run more efficiently or provide better quality products to your customers. Because of these limiting factors, black-owned businesses often start out behind the eight ball.

Now, of course, we all have the right to spend our money however and wherever we choose, but to support black-owned businesses means that as black consumers we understand their challenges and can be sympathetic within reason. This also speaks to what we discussed in the first two chapters. Everyone is not equipped to run a business. The challenges are already stacked high against even the most competent business owners, leaving those less qualified business owners to the slaughter.

As a black business owner, you need to understand the correlation between an efficient cash flow cycle and good customer service. The two variables that are affected here are the availability of product and pricing. Both are affected by hindering external factors, but with proper planning, they both can be overcome. There is a certain level of understanding that is required to solve this equation, and when you add in "the black factor", the equation becomes even more difficult to solve.

So how do we solve it? I don't think there is a single answer. For starters, it will take extreme due diligence, insightful mentorship and inclusion. Unfortunately, black business owners are typically not included in those networking ecosystems that offer valuable business resources. Having sound mentorship in the beginning stages of your business can give you the tools needed to navigate through the rugged business world. I'm pretty sure the next question you are thinking is "How do I find a good mentor?" Well, I am so glad you asked! Finding a mentor may seem challenging, but it doesn't have to be. Here are a few tips to help you get started on your mentorship journey.

1. Know What You Want

Before engaging in your mentorship journey, make sure that you know what you are looking for in a mentor. Are you looking for help with financing? Are you struggling with employees? Do you need marketing advice? Understanding what your needs are will make this process a little less daunting. Being prepared will also show your potential mentor that you are serious.

2. Ask and You Shall Find

Start by looking at successful business owners that you may know from your community or church, but be sure to do your own due diligence. Research them online, read their reviews and determine if they have established a proven track record. Make sure that their goals align with yours. Find out if they have knowledge of the industry or business you are pursuing. Don't be afraid to ask for mentorship. Oftentimes pride may prevent us from asking for help, but in the business world, that type of pride can be detrimental to your success. Lean into the expertise of those that walked the path before you. Learning about their mistakes is just as valuable as knowing about their successes. Keep in mind that the first person you approach may not be the right fit—but don't worry, most people would be happy to refer you to colleagues or other business associates that may be a better fit.

3. Networking

In almost every city or county there are groups and organizations dedicated to small businesses. Consider joining one or more of these professional organizations. This is great if you have an already established business, but if you are in the beginning stages of your business and have not yet launched, you may need to stash this tip in your back pocket for now! Groups like the Chamber of Commerce are a great place to start. There are also many Chamber of Commerce organizations dedicated specifically to the African American demographic. Whatever group piques your interest, be sure to engage with professionalism and sincerity.

4. SBA

The Small Business Administration has tons of resources dedicated to help with the success of small business owners. Programs like SCORE can help connect business owners with suitable mentors. These partnerships can be very insightful in areas such as marketing and finance. You will have to do the research to see what agencies are available in your particular area.

5. Explore Diversity

There could be times that you may need advice or mentorship specific to black issues and having an African American mentor may be the best option to help you navigate those cultural issues that may affect your business. On the other hand, you may at times need to explore those diverse mentorships that can potentially give you access to information and resources that you would not normally have access to through regular channels. Sometimes we may overlook opportunities because we may be intimated or suspicious of working with those individuals that may not look like us. However, if you are going to succeed, you have to understand that everyone that does not look like you is not necessarily your enemy. Don't be too quick to dismiss or discount potential beneficial collaborations because of your own predetermined biases.

Perhaps one of the biggest takeaways of your mentorship journey is to always be sure to respect and value any mentor or potential mentor's time. As you know, time is a resource that most successful business owners hold in high regard. If they take the time out of their busy schedule to share advice, make sure that you are prepared. Show gratitude for their time by being respectful and open minded.

CHAPTER 5

Look the Part. Live the Part.

O kay, so now you have decided to take the idea of owning a business seriously. Now what? For starters, let's scrap all of the crazy ambitious ideas and start with a few basics. There are 16 key questions that you must ask yourself, so ready that paper and pen and prepare to assess yourself...and be honest!

1. Do you have experience running a business?
2. Do you have customer service experience?
3. Are you prepared to learn the necessary skills it takes to run a business?
4. Do you have the time to run a business?
5. Have you saved enough money to start a business?
6. Is your credit rating strong enough to obtain financing?
7. Have you created a business plan?
8. What is your motivation behind you starting a business?
9. What problem does your product or service solve?
10. Who will your customers be?
11. How will you service them?
12. Are there others providing the same service in your market?
13. Are you confident that you will be able to compete with them and be profitable?
14. What are your weaknesses when it comes to running a business?

Of course there are hundreds of questions you can ask yourself, but we will start with these basic few for now. Take a moment to review your answers. Did you answer no to the majority of these key questions? If you did, then you may want to reconsider the path you are about to go down and stick to being a hobbyist. However, if you are willing to learn and put forth the effort, then trek away my friend; it can be a very rewarding experience!

The first thing you want to think about is what kind of business structure is right for you. For most mom and pop-sized businesses, a sole-proprietorship or a single member LLC may be a good option. If you have more ambitious goals and plan on having partners and board members, then a partnership or a corporation may be the right fit. Whatever the case may be, the best thing to do is to consult an accountant and a lawyer to see which option is best suited for your particular needs. Just know that there are certain levels of protection that each entity may provide or not provide, so be sure to keep that in mind before you start selling those plates out of your residential kitchen. If someone gets sick from your food, you could be personally held liable if you are not properly structured for protection. You could also be facing serious fines for not meeting health inspection standards and requirements. You see how fast things can spiral out of control? Once you leave the hobbyist world and enter into the business domain, you must realize that you expose yourself to certain liabilities that may carry heavier penalties if you do not do things the right way.

After you have determined which business structure is best for your business, the next thing you want to think about is the name of the business. It is a basic but important part of laying a solid foundation for your business. It is also the cornerstone of your brand.

So...what is a brand and why is it important? According to Merriam Webster dictionary, a brand is defined as a public image, or identity conceived of as something to be marketed or promoted. I know it seems like a lot to unpack, but don't worry I will connect the dots in just a moment, but first I want to revisit something I mentioned earlier.

Remember that EIN we talked about? Here is why it is important to you. An EIN (Employer Identification Number) or TIN (Taxpayer Identifier Number) is a unique nine-digit number that identifies your specific business for tax purposes. You may also use your social security number if you are planning to operate as a sole proprietor or a single member LLC, but again, I strongly recommend discussing your specific situation with your accountant or attorney to ensure that you are making the best decision for your business.

Now...back to why this number is so important. An EIN is typically required to open business bank accounts, file taxes, apply for business loans, and even take advantage of special pricing from certain wholesalers. So how does all of this tie into customer service? It's simple. All of these things help to build trust in your brand and establish credibility for your business within the public's eye. It feels pretty weird when you are doing business with someone who is supposed to be operating as a business, but can only receive a cash payment or a check made out in their personal name. For some people, that may be okay, but here is a word of caution. Most businesses that spend real money will not look to do any business with a company that cannot provide a viable EIN number or business banking account number. Imagine this. Company XYZ is in the middle of reviewing their quarterly audit when their auditor notices a payment to Joseph Somebody. Big companies try to avoid any questionable transactions that may put them at risk.

A good public image is the cornerstone of any brand or business's long-term success. A good reputation is the foundation on which good customer service is built. When a potential customer looks at the name of your business, your website, or even your logo, they will immediately know if they feel comfortable doing business with you. If your logo looks like you went with the first thing you scribbled on a napkin, most people will automatically view your brand as inferior. Oh yeah, make sure that you invest in a quality logo. It matters.

Now that you understand how to look the part, you need to live the part. Build on the foundation that you have laid and make your brand mean something. Take accountability for all of it, the good and the bad. If your website sucks because most of the links never work, it's your fault. Own it. Correct it. Invest in quality to make your customer's experience awesome. First impressions are everything and that's the one thing you need to realize *sooner* than later.

Once you have the foundation laid for your business, there are a few other ideas you may want to consider and surprisingly they all will not break the bank. Let's take a quick look at some of the things you should be focusing on now.

Website

In today's world a website is a "must have" and not a "nice to have". If you don't have an active up-to-date website, you are putting your business at a serious disadvantage and you are doing your customers a major disservice. Consumers have become accustomed to having immediate access, and if you can't give them that on the most basic level, you've lost them. A website helps build your credibility and puts your customer's mind at ease. You're visible. You're accessible. In the eyes of the customer, you're not going to disappear with their money in the middle of the night, at least not without some kind of visible trail.

There are many services that offer basic web pages with templates and cheap hosting. Sites like Wix and Squarespace make it easy for beginners to create a basic functioning website. It's usually free to establish an account and free to build a website, but you may need to pay a nominal monthly hosting fee to maintain the site. In some cases, when using the free version of some website builders, your website might be subject to watermarks clearly indicating that you are using the free version. That may not seem like a big deal, and it may not be a big deal if you are just starting out and it's the only option available; however, some customers may look at that as a red flag. Think about it. If anyone can log on and create any website in five minutes, what's stopping a shyster from doing the same thing? Shelling out the few extra bucks a month will totally be worth it because it lends more credibility to your website and your brand. There are other platforms, such as Wordpress, that offer a fair amount of customization and functionality. Depending on your needs, it may be worth the time to fully investigate the different offerings and compare them against your needs.

Another important thing worth mentioning is your website address. You know www.something.com. Think long and hard before settling in on a particular URL. Once it's out there, it will be hard to change down the road, so make sure that you take time to research available domain names, and make every best effort to choose a name that is catchy, easy to remember, but most importantly, relevant to your business.

Email

Okay, here is where I might have some biased opinions. But it's okay… it's not personal, it's only business. And that is exactly why you need a business email address! Using johnlives4fun@gmail.com (it's not a real email) for your business is absolutely one of the worst things you can do. Just like a website, a formally structured email address such as john@somerealbusiness.com is what you need to help strengthen your business's credibility. If your personal gmail is on your business card today, you get a pass, but if you hand that card out tomorrow, shame on you. Similarly to websites, you will probably have to pay a small monthly fee to maintain your custom email account, but again, it's well worth it to be able to look more professional.

Telephone

It is certainly tempting to slap your cell phone number on a business card and start passing them out like candy at a parade. In some cases, that may be the only telephone number you have. It's easy, convenient, and will almost certainly cause problems for you down the road. The biggest thing to take away here is this...keep your personal and business telephone numbers separate! You will thank me later.

A telephone number gives a person access. When you give a customer your personal cell phone number, you are giving them the perception that you are accessible anytime. If you are working with high value clients, then this may be something that makes sense; however, you should still get a separate cell phone to conduct that type of high-end priority business. Having a dedicated business telephone number sets boundaries and establishes the parameters in which customers can expect to have access to service.

Here's an example. Suppose it's Saturday morning and a customer calls you with an issue. Normally, you don't accept business calls on Saturdays because it's the day you spend with the kids, but the customer doesn't know that. Of course, you could update your voicemail every day to keep your customers informed of your availability, but you run the risk of looking unprofessional.

Have you ever called a business at 1 AM in the morning just to see if they would answer? I know I have. Typically you would receive an answering message and sometimes you may actually get a live person, depending on the company's investment in a call center. Usually, if I call a business and it sounds like I am calling a personal number, I get suspicious. I am typically looking to hear something like: "Hello, thank you for calling ABC company. How may we help you?" or even, "Thank you for calling ABC company. We are currently closed, but please feel free to call back during our normal business hours." That is a totally acceptable voicemail.

When I call a company, I am not looking for a simple hello. I'm expecting the beginning of my customer experience to be amazing, but more importantly, to gain my trust. Your personal telephone number should be reserved only for your most valuable customers. In fact, having your personal number should make them feel special. In this case, you have earned their business and their trust enough to move your relationship to the next level. If everyone has your cell number, how will your most valuable customers feel special?

Like everything else, there are always solutions out there to solve these kinds of problems. Some options are expensive, but there are many reasonable VoIP solutions for you to consider. Here are a few to consider:

Vonage
Grasshopper
Nextiva
Godaddy
Phone.com
Google Voice

A VoIP or Voice over Internet Protocol is a technology that lets anyone place phone calls over an internet connection. These options can be a great alternative to landlines or additional cell phones. In fact, they may have lower monthly costs and come with more features. Some of these features may include 800 numbers, custom extensions, and custom hold music. All of these features will help your brand stand out and separate you from the amateurs.

Business Cards

Business cards are the most basic form of advertising and can be used in customer service interactions as well. The first thing you must do is make sure that you have quality, professional looking business cards. I would be remiss if I didn't share a story about the time I was handed a business card that had handwritten smeared ink on the face of the card. At first I thought it was a joke, but quickly realized this individual was as serious as a heart attack, or at least they intended to be. Needless to say, the card got tossed in the trash almost immediately. To this day, I don't remember the business or the service they offered. Now do you see why brand matters? It's those little things that stand out when you only have one chance for a first impression. If you're a business, act like business. If you have a side hustle, don't try to act like a business.

Business cards can also be used in those customer service situations where an issue needs to be escalated and giving your business card to that customer as a key point of contact may actually help diffuse the situation or resolve the issue. When a customer has an issue, one of the worst things you can do is have them calling and emailing ten different people in order to get a resolution to their problem. Your business card in its basic design should have the following:

Your Brand Logo
Your Company Name
Your Name
Your Title
Your Business Telephone Number
Your Business Email Address
Your Company Website
Your Company Address (if applicable)

Having a professional business card does two things. One, it puts the customer at ease and lets them know that they are dealing with a professional company, and two, it gives them a single point of contact, reassuring them that this one person will be helping them resolve any issues. Who would have thought that a 3.5 x 2-inch card would be so important? There are many places to get professional business cards printed, so you really have no excuse not to have quality cards at your fingertips.

Vistaprint is a popular printing company known for quality as well as reasonable pricing. Of course there are always stationary stores such as Staples, but let's not forget about those local community printers either. Oftentimes, they have great products and have special offers for other neighborhood business owners. You can also browse the web for some great printers that offer high quality printing at reasonable prices.

Social Media

Okay, here is where my age shows a bit. A few years back, I was at an event and someone asked for my contact information. Naturally, I handed them a business card out of habit, but this was a younger someone and they looked totally confused. They asked me what's my Instagram name, and I looked like a deer in headlights. I simply informed them that I had not set up an Instagram account and handed them my card anyway. The ironic thing is that I felt like I handed them a card with handwritten smeared ink. That was a lesson learned that I am happy to share with you.

You have to be prepared to meet your customers where they are. In today's world, almost everyone is on social media. They connect there, they engage there, and lots of people do business there. Let's face it, this digital stuff is not going away so we can embrace it or get left behind.

If you haven't already, I would strongly suggest that you create a brand or business social account on all the major social media platforms. These accounts should be separate from your personal accounts. The account handles should match the name of your brand or business or they should at least be relatively close. Be sure to only post business related content on these pages.

One way to incorporate your social media into your business card is to have QR codes printed on one side of your business card. You can program your QR codes with links to your social media pages. This is a great way to make sure that you can stay connected to all of your customers.

There are also a lot of cool digital business card platforms available with pretty reasonable pricing. Platforms like switchitapp.com allow you to add videos and social media to a shareable link. At the end of the day there are tons of ways to share your information. The takeaway here should be that no matter which method you choose, be sure that it is professional and relevant to your business.

CHAPTER 6

Why Brand is Everything...

Why do people buy Apple computers when they can buy significantly cheaper brands and models? Why would a person buy a Mercedes-Benz when they can buy a budget vehicle that accomplishes the same thing? Why do people sit in the long drive through lines at Chick-Fil-A, when they could easily go somewhere else to get a chicken sandwich? The answer is service. People know that Apple stands by their product. If you have ever purchased an Apple Care plan, you know that you will receive stellar customer service. People that own a Mercedes know that when they take their car in for servicing, they not only get a nice luxury loaner, they know that when they get their car back, it will be clean and detailed and almost like new. People will wait over twenty minutes to purchase a meal at Chick-Fil-A because they know they are going to get five-star customer service at any location they visit.

No matter which Apple store, Mercedes-Benz dealership, or Chick-Fil-A restaurant you patronize, the cardinal principle remains the same...excellent and consistent customer service. People will pay more to be treated well. They value good customer service, and are willing to pay a premium price, even if the product is average. Remember, products and services are expendable, but a good brand promotes confidence and trust, two things that will keep customers buying from you. However, this by no means implies that your products and services can be inferior!

If your products and services are subpar, your brand will suffer quickly. Most people can be forgiving if they have a poor customer experience here and there, but almost everyone will draw the line at spending their hard earned money on a below average product or service!

Once you have solidified your brand within a market, you automatically increase the value of your business, but you should be fair-warned, it takes a lot of work to build your brand up to that level, and it's something you should be thinking about in the beginning stages of your business.

Now that we have established the importance of branding, you should also be thinking about how one little customer service blunder can send your brand spiraling into the abyss of the ubiquitous cancel culture. Your brand is your promise to your customers. Your brand tells your customers what they can expect from you whenever they spend their hard-earned paycheck on your products and services. If you break that promise, it will be hard for them to trust your brand again. Customer service should always be tied to brand, whether it's through your brand promise, mission statement, or overall company vision. As you can see, customer service and branding are closely relatedly. A strong brand can help set expectations and create a positive perception of the customer experience, ultimately leading to increased customer loyalty and ultimately adding to your bottom line!

CHAPTER 7

The Power of Process

The most successful organizations in the world understand that success is based on systems and processes. The Merriam-Webster Dictionary defines a **system** as an organized set of doctrines, ideas, or principles usually intended to explain the arrangement or working of a systematic whole. It further defines a system as being an organized or established procedure.

The Merriam-Webster Dictionary defines a **process** as a series of operations conducing an end. Let's take a moment to unpack this. The word conducing means to lead or tend to a particular and often desirable result. When we examine the definition of the word process while looking at it in context, we can safely assume that process simply means one would need to establish a series of operations in order to achieve a desirable result. The Merriam-Webster Dictionary also defines the word **operation** as the performance of a practical work or of something involving the practical application of principles and or processes. This simply means that you, as a business owner, must develop a practical process or system around customer service. Process helps to establish consistency. It also helps shape the credibility of your brand.

A well thought out system will help alleviate the need for you to become emotional when dealing with a challenging customer service issue. Of course, there will be times when you will need to make judgment calls and deviate from your system; however, when you do, you should have already evaluated the financial and perceptual ramifications of doing so. A sound system will help you evaluate a situation and respond in a professional and non-emotional way. Customer service may be all about empathy, but at the end of the day, it's still about business. Is refusing to refund twenty dollars really worth all of the negative publicity a bad online review will bring? Or would you rather eat the twenty dollars and receive rave online reviews potentially worth hundreds or even thousands of dollars in free positive publicity?

A good system will also help you to maintain consistency around common sense decision making and empower your employees to be good stewards of your business. By giving them the tools they need to make those decisions, you alleviate the need for them to feel stressed when faced with challenging customer issues. These tools may come in the form of store policies which may provide a standard of reasonable thresholds that allow your employees to evaluate, measure, and decide without any additional pressure. They can lean on these policies whether you are there or not, but more importantly, it will provide a consistent and enforceable response for every customer interaction. Just remember that it is your job to ensure that your staff understands your company's policy and the philosophies that prompted the system you created. Keep in mind that "attitude" should not impact the process. In fact, the only acceptable attitude is a good attitude.

A solid process is something that you will develop over time. You should also expect your process to evolve over time as well. Now I am quite sure you're all wondering what your process should look like, right? Well to be honest and fair, everyone's process will be different. It will look different. It will feel different and it will function different.

For example, let's say that you run a bookkeeping service. Your process around customer service will be much different than a person that runs a bakery. You know (or at least you should know) that tax season is always a busy time for you. You should be planning to hire additional bookkeepers and customer service representatives to help with the influx of work during that busy time. A baker may need to hire additional help in the spring, summer and fall because most of their business comes from weddings and other events occurring during those particular seasons.

A bookkeeper will need to hire well qualified and skilled individuals because accounting mistakes can potentially cost them their reputation. While friendliness is a pillar of good customer service, a book keeper's client may measure good customer service by the accuracy and timeliness of their tax documents. A baker on the other hand may not necessarily need skilled labor; but they may need someone that can handle anxious customers that come into the shop. A baker's customer may need more compassion and empathy as they help guide their patrons through choosing the best cake for a personal and emotional time in their lives.

As you can see, each business need is different. Each business has a different requirement and you need to be an expert when it comes to knowing what your business requires to deliver great customer service.

Exercise

Here is an exercise that may help you determine where to begin in your process. You have to ask yourself a few basic questions so that you can uncover a truthful assessment of your needs. Here are some key questions to consider.

- "What do my customers expect from my business?"
- "What would my customers think is an acceptable level of service?"
- "Am I currently capable of delivering that level of service or better?"
- "Are my product and service guarantees realistic?"
- "Are my current refund policies clear and visible?"
- "How do my customers feel about these policies?"
- "Can my current business cash flow handle my refund policies?"
- "What is my escalation process?"

Answering these questions will give you a general idea on where to begin. Ideally, you will want to work backwards. Put yourself in your customer's shoes and walk through one of your business's standard transactions. (Trust me, it will help!) Write down all of the things that probably went well from the beginning of the transaction to the end of the transaction. How did you feel at the end of the transaction? It might seem hypothetical, but the mind can be a powerful tool once you put it to work. Imagine what that experience felt like. Were you satisfied? Were you thanked for your business? Did anyone assist you with your purchase? Did you understand what you were buying? Did you need it? Did you want it?

Take inventory of all your answers and set them aside for now. Next, think about all of the things that potentially could have gone wrong and write your answers down. Was your facility untidy? Did you run out of inventory? Was your staff unfriendly? Was your credit card machine down? Did you understand what you were buying and if it was returnable?

Be detailed and honest in your assessment. Every variable matters. If you have the resources, feel free to recruit a few good friends to help you complete this recon mission. As a business owner, you need to look at your current process with a jaundiced eye, and be willing to own and accept the good and the bad. This exercise is designed to make you internalize your current process from a customer's point of view.

Now that you have all of this intel, what do you do now? The first thing you do is congratulate yourself for all of the things that you got right. Hard work deserves a moment of praise, but only a brief moment. Now it's time to roll up those sleeves and go to work on the bad.

First, you should outline all of the areas that you found were lacking. Using a red pen, write them all down in sequential order. For example, if no one greeted you at the beginning of your transaction, put it at the top of the page. If an employee was unfriendly, write it somewhere in the middle. You basically want to build a timeline that reflects every point of your customer service process from beginning to end. After you've written all the bad things down, go back and fill in all of the good things using blue ink. You should now be able to visually see the complete picture based on this timeline. These are what I call your core behaviors.

Next, take a look at the first red item. On a separate page, write that behavior as your title. Take a deep breath and think about how you can improve on it. For example, if your store was untidy when you walked in, what can you do to improve this? You might consider creating a routine cleaning schedule for your employees to adhere to or you may need to hire an external cleaning company.

If your lines were outrageously long and your employees were extremely slow on the registers, what are you going to do about it? You may need to evaluate each employee's skill set and consider shuffling personnel around. People that are in charge of handling your customer's experience and handling your money need to be top notch. It may seem harsh, but this should be non-negotiable. If you don't have the best people representing your business on the front lines, then you could soon be out of business.

Once you have pages filled with those red titles, repeat the process for all of the good stuff, but this time, think of ways you can expand on how you can do things even better without changing those good core behaviors.

Now that you have taken the time to think through some viable solutions to improve your process, grab a binder and place all of those pages inside, keeping them in their sequential order. This is now your process bible. These are your core behaviors that will drive your customer experience from beginning to end. The next step involves trial and error. Remember all of those great ideas? Some will work and some will not. Keep the ideas that work and make them a standard practice. Of course this will take time, but you will now have a foundation on which to build on.

Will this binder save you from every issue or nuanced situation? Of course not. This is only the first step in creating a loosely automated platform that your business can run on whether you are there or not. As the business owner, you need to standardize this process and make it the law that ultimately comes with consequences for not adhering to them.

But wait a minute…this is all great stuff if you run a brick-and-mortar store right? But what if you run an online business? Or what if you have a home-based business?

How can you approach this recon exercise and get the intel needed to help your web or home-based business? The good thing is, the process is no different, except you may save a few bucks on gas.

Invite a few trust-worthy friends to engage in a few transactions on your website. (If you are a home-based business and don't have a website, stop now and go back to Chapter 5 now!)

It might not hurt to comp a few products or offer them gift cards to make it worth their time. Ask them to document their experience from the moment they log onto your site all the way until the end of their transaction. In this case, the employees are replaced by a UI (user interface) and the customer experience is impacted by functionality. Here are some additional questions to consider.

"Are your products or services clearly explained to the user?
"Is your website easy to navigate?
"Does it appear trustworthy?
"Did you feel like your transaction was secure?
"Were your policies visible and clear?"
"Was there an option to chat or speak to a live representative?"
"Was there a way to contact you if something went wrong?"

These are just a few questionable scenarios that your "spies" should be on the lookout for. Once you have all of your intel, you can complete all of the same steps I mentioned earlier, just keep in mind that some of your solutions may be more technical than practical.

CHAPTER 8

Planning to Fail

One of the keys to running a successful business is thinking about and developing a plan to fail. Our trusty dictionary tells us that the word "fail" means to stop functioning normally or to become absent or inadequate. Let's face it, failure is a natural part of life, even when it comes to our health. That is the very reason most people, if it is in their means, try to acquire some kind of health care. They know something will go amiss with their health at some point in their life and they simply want to be prepared to handle it when it does. This same philosophy should apply to your business health as well.

Contingency should become a regular part of your vocabulary. You should always be in a constant state of "what if?" Although I am speaking literally, I am not implying that you dive into a deep state of paranoia; however, a small degree of discomfort is always a good thing.

Remember the process that you worked on in the last chapter? Well, here is where you get to break open that binder and throw darts at every aspect of your newly developed process. Analyze each section and try to come up with different scenarios in which something could go wrong. Think about what would happen if there was a power outage. What happens if a delivery is late? What will you do if you unexpectedly sell out of your most popular product? What happens when two of your employees call out sick on a busy weekend?

All of these are real-life scenarios that could actually happen. The question is, will you be prepared, or will you let the situation spiral out of control and leave a blemish on your reputation? This is why it is important to develop an "insurance plan", in the event something goes wrong. After all, it is your responsibility to maintain a seamless customer experience.

Not only should you be thinking about all of the things that can go wrong, you need to be thinking about viable solutions as well. There is a reason people will pay for extended warranties on their automobiles. They know it's a matter of "when" and not "if".

What does this look like for your business? Well, it all depends on what type of business you are running and what your operational needs are. For example, if you are running a restaurant, then you should always be looking for vendors and suppliers that can provide consistent quality products. If your best-selling dish is chicken cacciatore, it would be quite disappointing if your regular customers drive all the way to your restaurant only to find out that you don't have any chicken because your supplier had an unforeseen issue. You need to be constantly working on a plan B, C, D, and E...at all times! You should always have a backup supplier...and a backup supplier to that backup supplier.

Have you ever been to a mom and pop auto-mechanic? A lot of times when they diagnose a problem, they tell you that they can fix the problem, but they have to order the part and it will take a few days for the part to get there. Compare that to a larger retail auto mechanic that has access to multiple suppliers and they can get the part in a couple of hours. It may cost you a little bit more, but they can have you back on the road in a few hours versus a few days.

Some small businesses fall into the first category where they are dependent on a single supplier relationship for whatever reason. Maybe it's the only supplier in town. Maybe they don't have the business credit to open multiple wholesale accounts. Maybe they are not legally established as a credible business and are not eligible for a purchasing account. Whatever the case may be, having a lack of available resources to support your business needs is a real obstacle. It is critical that you think ahead and try to hedge any potential issues or threats to your process. In some cases, some of these pitfalls can be avoided with proper planning.

Take a few moments to think about the needs of your business. What are the top key problems that could bring your process to a halt? If you are a caterer, would running out of aluminum pans be an issue? If you run a restaurant, would running out of forks or napkins cause grief to your customers? If you have a moving company, how disruptive would a couple of trucks needing sudden repair be to your daily operation? How many customers would you have to turn away? How many customers would be angry? How many customers will walk away blurting out that they will never support another black-owned business again?

One way of avoiding a first-class invitation to the blackballed black business club is to anticipate the most common inevitable issues and prepare a series of contingency plans. The truth is...stuff happens. It's the way life is and it's the way business is. Coming out of these mishaps successfully can be achieved if you, the business owner, can be proactive instead of reactive. Here are a few more ideas to help keep you ahead of the game.

1. Evaluate all of the key products and/or services required to keep your business operating on a routine basis. Make a list of backup suppliers, wholesalers, and vendors that can effectively keep your supply chain going without missing a beat.
2. While thinking about all of the worst-case scenarios, also think about some kind of compensating award for your customers if you are unable to correct a problem in a timely fashion. When issues arise, they may not always be your fault, but offering your customers a little something for their inconvenience goes a long way. Consider offering a gift card or possibly a discount on a future purchase. Make sure that your customers know that this is not a routine screw up and that you are already ahead of the situation. Usually, customers get

edgy when there is a problem and the business owner takes a blind eye, willfully or otherwise.

3. Apply for a line of credit. Now, before you get excited, keep in mind that these funds should **only be used for actual emergency situations.** Those situations that may require an emergency repair, or those instances where you may need to pay additional costs for express shipping to ensure your product arrives on time. If you are having trouble getting a line of credit, be sure to routinely put money aside into an emergency savings account. Having access to funds when you need to correct an issue promptly is paramount. There is nothing worse than having customers sweltering in your establishment because you don't have the funds to fix the air conditioning unit.

Be sure to communicate your contingency plans with your team. When a problem arises, you will need all hands on deck. Be aware that your team, staff, or crew will be taking their cues from you. Everyone should be aware that they have an active role in problem resolution and their primary goal is to achieve customer satisfaction.

CHAPTER 9

Is the Price Right?

re people complaining about your prices? Are they telling you that your prices are too high? Are they threatening to take their business elsewhere because "they can get it cheaper"? Guess what...all businesses go through this. Some shoppers are driven by price...period. Some consumers feel like they deserve to get a deal on every transaction. Some customers will think they deserve the hook up because both consumer and seller are black. At some point you will face one of these scenarios and there is nothing you can do about it.

As I briefly mentioned in the chapter "The Unbalanced Equation", black-owned businesses don't always have access to buy products at wholesale prices for various reasons. This is a legitimate variable that may affect your pricing structure and you will need to find a way to navigate through your particular market and mitigate this particular obstacle. The question you have to ask yourself is "how do I remain competitive without sacrificing all of my profit, while maintaining a stellar level of customer service"? It may seem impossible, but don't worry— it is doable!

The first thing you have to do is condition your mind. Begin by asking yourself the following questions.

- Are my prices the lowest they can be at the moment?
- Am I buying at a reasonable wholesale price?
- Am I still making a profit?

- Has my pricing been consistent?
- Are my products and services reasonably and competitively priced
- within my market?
- Do I have a plan in place for price changes?
- Are my products and services distinguished enough for me to charge premium pricing?

If you answered yes to ALL of these questions, rest easy, you are on the right track...for now. If you answered no to ANY of these questions, you really need to examine your pricing structure more closely.

So what did I mean by conditioning your mind? Similar to the popular serenity prayer, you have to learn to accept the things that you cannot change or control. This includes frugal customers, market shifts, changing regulations, and the price of materials. These particular variables affect entire industries and are not specific to your business alone. Customers will gripe at price changes stemming from these factors, but they will eventually accept it and life will move on. However, customers will not tolerate sporadic price changes or unfair price gouging. Inconsistent pricing is a sure way to end up in the middle of a triggered customer service cancel culture campaign.

The reality is...prices change. It's the nature of business. It's the nature of supply and demand. It's the nature of rising costs of raw materials. Consumers expect price change within reason and because of this, you need to have a plan around when and how you communicate your price changes to your customers.

One of the most frustrating things a customer can experience is making a purchase (or even window shopping) at an establishment one day, only to return a couple of days later to a higher price tag. This situation might be justified if a particular item was on sale and the sale has now ended; however, this needs to be communicated clearly and concisely. Nothing screams "shady" more than fluctuating prices without rhyme or reason.

From observation and experience, here are a few bad habits that can get you into trouble.

1. You have not established a standard pricing list or pricing table.
2. You have not established a schedule for routine price increases.
3. You don't know or understand your profit margins.
4. You fail to continually seek competitive wholesale pricing.

If you are guilty of any of these habits on this list, shame on you, but it's okay; you have the opportunity to turn things around. The first thing you need to do is examine your current pricing schedule. You should be able to accurately explain in detail the products and services you provide and the costs associated with those products and services. This should be regarded as your pricing bible. There should never be a situation where you have to guess what your pricing is. By establishing a solid pricing structure, you ensure that your customers will receive fair and consistent pricing. You also ensure that you are able to accurately forecast sales pipelines and predict potential revenue.

It's been a running joke, especially with some black-owned businesses, that prices change with the business owner's monthly bills. I've heard this particular sneer aimed at beauty and hair salons specifically. Your customers are not dense. They can sense when something is not quite right when it comes to shelling out their hard-earned money. Inconsistency leads to a bad customer experience. Bad customer experiences lead to loss of revenue.

The cost of doing business is almost certain to increase every year. A good rule of thumb is to plan for routine price increases. You may want to consider announcing your price increases at the end of the year, in preparation for the new year. For example, you can inform your customers that prices will increase starting January 1, but you do this in November or December of the previous year. This gives your customers plenty of time to prepare for and embrace the upcoming price change.

You need to remember that clear communication and transparency is key. Be upfront and honest about price increases. Call them what they are. Don't sugarcoat or downplay the true nature of what is happening. Own it. Your prices are increasing because you need to make sure that you will remain in business to serve your customers. Communicate price increases with a truthful and valid explanation. Most customers will understand the rising cost of business, so tell them that. If you needed to make improvements on your building, or perhaps buy another truck or expensive piece of machinery, customers will typically understand your justification, especially if it will mean a better customer service experience for them. Keep in mind that you should always take a *value-based narrative* approach. A value-based narrative is a compelling story that justifies a price increase by placing focus on the benefits the customer will receive because of that increase. By always keeping the customer experience at the forefront, your customers will feel valued and will embrace the price increase with minimum friction.

Here are some examples of how a value-based narrative can be used as a tool to communicate new prices.

"Our goal is to ensure that we are able to make your experience as pleasurable as possible. In order to ensure that we provide the best customer service experience, prices for our services will increase on [enter date] from [enter current pricing] to [enter new pricing]. While we strive to maintain fair and consistent prices, occasionally we find the need to increase prices accordingly as we make improvements so that we can continue to deliver the quality services that you deserve. We thank you in advance for your understanding."

Statements like this will keep the customer's mind on the inherent value of your service or product. The improvements you are making to your business will make a better overall experience for them, but here is the one big caveat. The improvements that you promised must be realized in a way that lines up with your customer's perception. A price increase with no perceivable benefit or value is a sure way to disrupt the customer experience, and negatively impact your brand.

CHAPTER 10

Where's the Ketchup?

Picture this. You've had a long day, you're hungry and you just want to grab some quick food and head home to kick back and catch up on your favorite shows. You pull into your favorite unhealthy fast-food restaurant and yell your order into the brightly colored menu board. Next, you pull up to the window, grab your bag and toss it into the passenger seat without checking your order. In fact, the high school worker wearing the radio on their head never even said thank you.

You make it home and finally dump your lukewarm food onto the snack tray in front of the television. As you settle in, you realize something. They never gave you any ketchup for your fries! How dare they! In my opinion, if you serve French fries or any kind of potato, ketchup should automatically come with the order...period! Is it a big deal? Possibly. It's not so much about the ketchup or lack thereof, it's the presumptuousness on the restaurant's part. In my opinion, it's borderline disrespectful. Condiments help enhance the eating experience. Fast food is meant to be comforting and pleasurable. If you enjoy ketchup on your fries (and I assume most people do), you now have to grab a cold bottle of ketchup from the fridge and dip your semi warm fries into a cold pool of thick clumpy ketchup. Yay.

Do you see how something as simple as excluding a few packets of ketchup can ruin the entire customer experience? To add insult to injury, the server never asked if I wanted ketchup. In situations like these, some things should be an automatic given. Now before I go on, I know that some of you bean counters are squirming in your seats. I know…restaurants have to cut costs. Food costs are rising. Margins are shrinking. I get it. Sometimes you have to cut costs and God forbid the shareholders or the business owners slice their profits. I totally understand the argument. Businesses are there to make money. But guess what…the money you make comes from hardworking customers. Without their hard-earned dollars flowing from their hands to your pockets, you would not be in business.

Customers don't know or care that food costs are rising. After all, that's your problem, not theirs, and because we live in a country driven by capitalism, the end user (the consumer) usually gets the short end of the stick. That simply means that you indirectly make your problems their problems by skimping on the cheese, using cheaper buns, and cheating them out of ketchup packets while charging them the same price if not more. Most people can see what's going on. They notice the smaller burger patty, and the smaller containers that their favorite sides are now packaged in. They most definitely notice. In some instances, I've seen restaurants put up signs informing the customer that ketchup will be given upon request. I honestly can't be mad at that because they at least give the customer a heads up about the situation.

Okay, my rant is over. In fact, the bigger picture has nothing to do with ketchup. The lack of ketchup packets is more of a representation of a blatant disrespect towards a loyal customer. By shafting us with the ketchup, you are ultimately telling us that making a profit is more important than our customer experience. Of course this may absolutely be the case, but your customers should never be made to feel the impact of that reality. Rising costs is something that you can't always prepare for; however, you should be intuitive enough not to get caught off guard. Okay, my digression is over. See you next chapter!

CHAPTER 11

Customer Service vs Customer Experience

Over the years the idea of customer service has certainly evolved. Some still refer to it as customer service while some have elevated the terminology to "the customer experience." Although the two ideas are similar, I believe there is a significant difference between the two. First, let's turn to our trusty Merriam-Webster dictionary to help us achieve some clarity.

According to Merriam-Webster, "service" is defined as employment as a servant; the occupation or function of serving; or the work performed by one that serves.

Merriam-Webster also defines "experience" as something personally encountered, undergone, or lived through. It also defines experience as the act or process of directly perceiving events or reality.

If you are following along closely, I hope you have noticed the difference. Based on the definition of service, one can conclude that customer service is something that you offer to your customer, you being the proprietor of course. Basically, you are offering to serve or provide a specified service to an individual or group of individuals that we commonly refer to as the customer. Hence, the onus is on you to provide the service to them. This implies that no effort from the customer is required.

Now when we talk about the customer experience, notice how the dynamic shifts. The customer must live through or become conscious of a series of events, meaning that the customer's involvement is absolutely necessary. By involvement, I am talking about your customer having the ability to process their engagement and develop an awareness that helps define or perceive their current emotional state. In order for there to be an experience, there has to be two things working simultaneously. You, the business owner, must provide a service, and the customer must receive your efforts in a manner that provokes a certain feeling.

The bottom line is that there is only one variable that you can truly control…the customer service that you provide. However, you can influence your customer's experience by providing extraordinary customer service. By being deliberate in your customer service delivery, you have the power to create a memorable experience that will leave your customers feeling elated.

So, I think the biggest takeaway here is this. Your ultimate goal should be focused on enhancing your customer's overall experience. How do you do that? By delivering unparalleled customer service. This means that you will have to go above and beyond what your competitors are doing. You have to set a higher bar for your staff. You have to do things that set yourself apart from everyone else. One of the easiest ways to do that is to practice empathy. Put yourself in your customer's shoes. What would make you feel appreciated? What would make you rave to your friends about the quality of the service you received? What was so amazing that you would automatically choose to use the service again? What made you say wow?

Of course, there is no magic answer. There is no "one size fits all" solution. To be successful, you will need to induce some serious out of the box thinking, followed up with an almost flawless execution. To help paint the picture even more clearly, let's look at an example on how that can work.

Assume you are the owner of a growing lawn care business. You are looking to grow your client base, but you are up against severe competition in your market. The first thing I would encourage you to do is perform some primary market research.

What are you specifically looking for? You're looking for any data that will provide clues that will ultimately help shape your customer's experience. You should at a minimum be looking for the following information.

- Who are your competitors?
- What is the pricing like in the area?
- Are some competitors charging a premium? Why?
- What are they offering that is different from everyone else in the market?
- What are customers saying in reviews about your competitors?
- What do the customers in your market consider valuable?

These simple questions should help you discover what potential customer service opportunities exist. For example, if you find a pattern of negative reviews around lateness and frequent cancellations, maybe you should focus on always being on time. Of course you need to ensure that you are able to deliver on that promise. My lawn care service does a good job of this by keeping me updated of any schedule changes. If they are running behind because of weather, they always send a text message with updates. This is a great way to stay ahead of any potential customer issues. What if I was planning to have a graduation party or a wedding reception in my yard? They at least give us the opportunity to let them know of such issues and they always find a way to fulfill our needs. There has never been a time where I had to guess when they would arrive to cut my lawn, and when they do show up, they always do a great job. Other lawn care services that I've had were not so impressive. The service was there, but the experience was not, hence the reason they were replaced. For me, I value good communication and good consistent work from my lawn care service, but other customers may value something totally different.

When perusing the reviews and the comments of your competitor's customers, be sure to look for those low hanging fruit opportunities. Not only should you be looking for the things they are doing wrong; you should be looking for the things they are not doing at all.

Here is an example. My family recently rescued a dog and yes, he is wonderful. We all love him unconditionally. What we don't love are the patches that he leaves in our lawn after he does his business. Is it a big deal? No. I'm not a lawn fanatic; however, if my lawn care service offered some tips, advice, or even a remedy around clearing up those brown patches, my customer experience would be elevated.

Another important principle that you have to understand is that customer service is reactive and a customer experience is proactive. With customer service, you are reacting to a particular customer need. In this example, I needed my lawn cut; however, a good customer experience is created when a customer's wants are fulfilled because the business owner has the foresight to fulfill that want. In this scenario, the lawn looks great; however, if the lawn care service notices the brown spots and offers remedies without being asked, the customer experience has just been elevated. See how that works? You solved a need that I didn't even ask for—yet desired.

By satisfying both needs and wants of the customer, you begin to create a solid customer service experience; however, if you are looking to create the ultimate customer experience, you will need to go a step further. You will need to exceed the customer's expectations. Think about this. Let's assume my lawn care service does an amazing job cutting my lawn. Let's even assume they've treated those brown spots and the grass is all turning back plush green again. Excellent! I'm winning as the customer. But wait! It gets even better. Once they have packed away their mowers and equipment, they leave a nice bag on my door with a $5 gift card to a local ice cream shop and a dog treat. Attached to the gift card is a note which reads:

Have some ice cream on us! We thought that you might want to have fun with your furry friend while enjoying your great looking lawn! It's going to be hot weather next week so here are some watering tips...

Okay. That would totally wow me! That is how you go above and beyond. They have created an unparalleled experience which allows me to:

1) enjoy my newly manicured lawn that I didn't have to cut myself

2) not worry about those ugly brown spots

3) enjoy a nice refreshing cone of ice cream while giving my furry friend a treat

4) utilize tips on how to maintain my lawn during hot weather

Not only did they exceed the service of other competitors in the area, they made it really difficult for me to even consider using anyone else for my lawn care. They have managed to turn me into a fan (but we will talk about that in another chapter). So, what is the second biggest takeaway from this chapter? You need to exceed your customer's expectations. Period.

But what happens when you slide towards the other side of the scale? You barely do a good job cutting the lawn and then you hurry to your next customer because you are trying to make your quota for the day. Your customers aren't happy with the way you edge their lawns. You leave grass clippings in the middle of the lawn, which eventually browns the surrounding grass. You said you were coming on Friday, but didn't show up until Monday with NO communication at all.

At this point, you are barely providing the basic customer service required to keep your customer satisfied. This type of behavior moves the focus away from the customer and it becomes more about the business. Once it becomes solely about the business, you are headed down a dark path. You need to realize that the focus should always be on the customer. Without the customer, you have no business. Of course you have to pay attention to payrolls, workloads, gas costs, and gross profits; however you need to perfect your customer service experience first!

CHAPTER 12

Basic Business Etiquette Part 1

There is an old saying that "please" and "thank you" go a long way; however, if you can begin a transaction with a smile followed by a genuine "How may I help you", you are on the path to winning at customer service. These foundational behaviors are the cornerstone of good business etiquette. What is business etiquette? Let's break it down!

Etiquette can be defined as the customary code of polite behavior in a society or among members of a particular profession or group. In this case, we are referring to business so we can safely assume that business etiquette is the customary code of polite behavior in business. Of course, the next logical question would be, what is the "customary code" and who determines what that code is? Merriam-Webster Dictionary defines customary as commonly practiced, used, or observed, so again we can safely deduce that the customary code of business etiquette refers to the commonly accepted customs, behaviors, and practices that are considered appropriate in a business setting.

Now that we have established a working knowledge of what business etiquette is, we can now take a closer look on how business etiquette and black-owned businesses intersect. The first thing we must realize is that business etiquette practices are not governed by legislation, but by standards put forth by a "progressive" society. I use the term progressive loosely because while it may be true that this country has made significant strides in the area of inclusion, we still fall short of being a truly equitable society. Why does this matter? It matters because the society in which we live is still plagued with biased ideologies rooted in racism and classism. As a society, we still struggle with divisive belief systems that transcend into all areas of our lives, including business.

The struggle for acceptance in today's society is real for African Americans. While inclusion exists to a nominal degree, African American business owners still struggle to find their place. Black business owners often find themselves held to the same business etiquette standards by a society that often fails to recognize them in a way that shows impartiality. In the same vein, black business owners are expected to adhere to the same high business etiquette standards, and to some degree, I agree. While specific customs and practices can differ between cultures, across industries, and even among specific communities, there are certain universal principles that guide business etiquette.

The determination of those principles can be influenced or motivated by several different factors including cultural customs, industry norms, and even technological advances such as social media. While there are some black-owned businesses astute enough to operate their business on a level that extends beyond the boundaries of the black community, there are many black-owned businesses that are confined to smaller communities. Because different businesses operate in different sized footprints, there are certainly notable differences in business etiquette practices. Those businesses that may operate on a national or global level will need to learn several different business etiquette practices.

For example, if conducting business in China, it is important for a company to be aware of the cultural norm of respecting authority. In Chinese business etiquette, it is customary for individuals to enter a room in hierarchical order. This means that when entering a room with your own teammates or when meeting potential business partners, it is recommended to follow this practice. Additionally, when addressing potential business partners, it is important to use proper titles to show respect. Addressing individuals by their appropriate titles reflects an understanding and acknowledgement of their status and position. This is a great example of cultural norms that dictate proper etiquette.

Now...let's refocus back on the smaller footprint, the black community. As a community, or society, what do our customers expect from business owners regarding business etiquette? For the most part, one would think that it's simply the same thing that everyone wants: to be treated with respect and dignity. While that does play a major part, it is not the only thing. Remember "the black factor" from a few chapters ago? Well, once again "the black factor" needs to be calculated into the business etiquette equation. Black consumers expect a lot more from black business owners in terms of business etiquette, and by rights they should.

Many black-owned businesses offer universal products and services, while some offer niche products and services targeted exclusively to black consumers. Those businesses offering universal products and services such as lawn care, plumbing, or maybe even janitorial services, will often subscribe to common business etiquette practices that are drawn from our quintessential American culture. Typical business etiquette is influenced by a combination of professional standards and certain general principles of business protocols that are widely observed by many. Here are what I consider to be the five key pillars of typical business etiquette that are fundamentally non-negotiable starters for any—and possibly all—customer service interactions.

1. A Professional Appearance

Looking the part is the first step in acting the part. Visual appearance is what customers see first and they will appreciate the extra effort in presenting yourself and your staff in an appropriate and respectable manner. In some cases, uniforms may be appropriate, and in other cases more professional attire may be more appropriate. In some instances, the casual approach may make sense. Specific dress codes may vary depending on the industry and organization and it is imperative that you understand the business etiquette climate you are in so that you and your team will appear professional, yet approachable.

2. Being on Time

Punctuality is often overlooked or even disregarded in the daily workflow of some black-owned businesses. Arriving on time for store openings, appointments, and other business commitments shows respect for others' time and exemplifies a certain level of professionalism.

3. Pleasant and Professional Greeting

All interactions should begin with a sincere smile, good eye contact, and a warm cordial greeting. A simple "May I help you?" or "How can I help you?" can potentially set the stage for a lucrative transaction. I cannot stress enough the importance of proper customer acknowledgement. This simple interaction will set the tone for everything that comes after.

4. Professional Communication

Any communication, whether verbal or non-verbal, should be approached in a respectful and appropriate manner. Professionalism and good business etiquette also extends to emails, social media, and any other digital communication. You should also be cognizant of your language and tone. Slang or any type of jargon may rub your customers the wrong way. Also, keep in mind it's not always what you say, but it's how you say it.

5. Be Respectful

In today's climate, everyone is looking for the slightest incident to make you the next poster child for cancel culture. Treating others with civility, professionalism, and inclusiveness regardless of their background or point of view is essential. You don't have to agree with every viewpoint and you don't need to win every argument. Be careful not to confuse your personal outlooks with your business goals. Of course, it may be likely that the two may converge at times, but it is critical that you temper your passions on topics that may offend your customers.

I know this may feel like elementary information; however, I am not taking for granted that everyone knows and adheres to the basics, otherwise, I would not have been compelled to write this book in response to the outcry of disappointment regarding customer service and black-owned businesses. In the next chapter, we will look a little more closely at some additional protocols that specifically black-owned businesses must embrace if they are truly going to satisfy the customer service needs of their primary customer base.

CHAPTER 13

Basic Business Etiquette Part 2

In the last chapter, we reviewed the basics of business etiquette, which surprisingly, many black-owned businesses frequently get wrong. Black-owned businesses play a crucial role in the economic growth and empowerment of African American communities. As these business owners attempt to find success, it is important that they learn to identify and embrace the unique expectations that African American consumers have regarding customer service. By recognizing and satisfying those expectations, black-owned businesses can cultivate strong customer relationships by delivering first-class customer service.

At the end of the last chapter, I mentioned "additional protocols" that black-owned businesses must be willing to embrace when specifically serving African American consumers. In addition to the business etiquette fundamentals, black-owned businesses must intentionally go a step further. Business etiquette for black-owned businesses undoubtedly transcends into a different kind of engagement that requires a true holistic approach. African American consumers often seek a sense of cultural understanding when engaging with black-owned businesses and more than likely will appreciate a business that goes the extra mile to celebrate their culture, history, and values.

African American consumers can be viewed as a society within a society, which means that they can and most likely will establish their own set of acceptable standards regarding business etiquette. If you haven't caught on by now, "the black factor" plays another influential role here. Research presented by McKinsey & Company revealed that black consumers demonstrate a greater inclination towards seeking and prioritizing brands that possess trustworthiness, social responsibility within the black community, and alignment with their cultural values. (1) So what does this have to do with business etiquette? This information gives us insight on what black consumers, by social convention, regard as acceptable expectations of good business behavior. Everything listed is in some way affected by the impact of customer service.

Customer service is the connective tissue that binds a business' brand with positive and measurable customer engagement, ultimately resulting in satisfied customers and a healthy bottom line.

By now you should be fully aware that African American consumers appreciate personalized and congenial customer service. They value businesses that take the time to understand their individual needs and preferences. They tend to appreciate a warm and inviting atmosphere, much resembling a safe haven from a world that values their money but not them. Business etiquette plays a pivotal role in helping to create that safe environment. When a black consumer enters your business, they expect to be greeted respectfully and pleasantly. By training your staff to say "May I help you?", you immediately set the tone for that customer's experience. Your staff should also be dressed in a presentable and professional manner. Of course, by the standards of mainstream America, this subject is treated objectively when the reality is, this is a totally subjective topic. For the most part, I believe that African American consumers are more likely to embrace people that look like them and dress like them; however, this does not mean that everything is acceptable. There is a fine line between being relatable and being offensive.

In recent news, there have been many arguments about certain "ethnic" hairstyles in the workplace. Luckily for black-owned businesses, this isn't a fallible issue. In fact, representation matters to African American consumers. They appreciate businesses that prioritize diversity and promote cultural experiences that resonate with their own heritage. By ensuring diverse representation, black-owned businesses can build trust, promote inclusivity, and create a welcoming environment.

Another thing to consider is that your customers come to your business to buy and your responsibility is to sell. Whether your goal is to make money or uplift your community by providing niche services and products, in every scenario, the onus is on the business to do a better job of selling than the buyer does of buying. I believe that black business owners often forget that the buyer has options and can choose to spend their money anywhere, hence they don't really *need* to buy from you unless you have a proprietary product or a monopoly in the marketplace. The flip side of this coin is that businesses actually need these customers to survive. In fact, you are at their mercy at all times so it behooves you not to take them for granted. Customers have options. Businesses don't necessarily have the same latitude. A customer can choose to leave your business and spend their money elsewhere. A business owner cannot necessarily guarantee they can readily find another consumer that is actually ready to buy. For this reason, it is super important that your business etiquette is polished enough to help guide your customers through a smooth transaction while they are primed to spend money. This also means that you and your staff need to be ready, willing, and able to answer any questions your customers may have about your products or services. This demonstrates a level of pride in your brand. Black consumers want to have trust in the products and services they are buying. If your salespeople are snappy, or demonstrate an inability or unwillingness to answer a question, then your customer's experience is ruined and their sentiment defaults to those all too familiar feelings of dismissal displayed by mainstream America.

African American consumers expect black-owned businesses to strive for excellence and maintain a high level of professionalism. This includes demonstrating strong business acumen, adhering to ethical standards, and offering exceptional customer experiences. Meeting and exceeding these expectations will contribute to a positive reputation and customer loyalty. Consistency in communication, timely responses to inquiries, and reliable delivery or service completion are crucial to creating that ultimate customer service experience.

One of the significant challenges is the presence of cultural biases and stereotypes that can impact customer service interactions. Unconscious biases may lead to assumptions or preconceived notions about African American customers or service providers which can hinder effective communication and create barriers to providing exceptional service. Overcoming these biases requires ongoing education, awareness training, and fostering a culture of inclusivity within the organization.

African American communication styles, which are often expressive and animated, may be misinterpreted or misunderstood by individuals from different cultural backgrounds. This misinterpretation can lead to miscommunication, confusion, or even offense. It is important for both service providers and customers to engage in active listening, patience, and a willingness to bridge cultural communication gaps.

CHAPTER 14

Perception is Reality

When I was working in banking, one of my managers used to always say this one phrase that always stuck in mind: Perception is reality. Why is a customer's perception important? Because everything a customer sees, hears, and feels during an interaction with your business is considered part of the customer experience. Your customer service performance is unfolding in the eyes of the customer in real time. From the greeting they hear when they enter your business doors, to the uniform they see when they first see your employees, all the way to the "Thank you and have a great day" they hear on the way out, your customers will remember every point of interaction...good and bad. Unfortunately, one bad interaction can potentially outweigh all of the good encounters during that one transaction and make your customer feel less than satisfied.

So what can you do? The best thing to do is make sure that you have a process in place that accounts for each potential point of interaction. You have to create an environment that "controls" the customer's perspective.

Here is an example of what that looks like:

Point 1: Upon entry, the customer is greeted with a smile and a warm welcome by an employee in proper uniform.

Point 2: The customer is asked if they need assistance (with a smile of course).

Point 3: During the sale, the employee asks if there is anything else they can assist with. This is also an opportunity to offer additional products or services. (We will talk about upselling and cross selling later.)

Point 4: The employee thanks the customer for their business.

Point 5: The customer receives a survey email or phone call or text asking how they rate their service and potentially offer them a coupon for future visits.

If you follow all the steps and touch all the points, you can see that every interaction with the customer has the potential to be positive. If by chance there is one fumble along the way, the impact may not be as severe because you will have had multiple positive impacts to negate the one negative interaction.

When it comes to black-owned businesses, we have already established that a customer's perception will be influenced by "the black factor". Some customers go in with a perceived notion that they are going to receive horrible service. However, some customers will go in with a hint of optimism and give the business the benefit of the doubt. In either case, there is an opportunity for you to shine.

According to the Merriam-Webster dictionary, the word "perception" means the result of perceiving or observation. The word "perceive" means to regard as being such. So how does this happen? It happens through experiences, both good and bad. It happens through word of mouth, social media posts, and online reviews. It happens when black-owned businesses are castigated for things that could have been prevented.

The good news is that perception can be influenced if you're willing to put in the work. The first thing you have to do is forget about everything you know and believe and look at things from the customer's point of view. Here is a fun activity that will help you do just that! The first thing you need to do is grab a disguise or a reliable friend and head on over to your business.

Level Up Exercise:

In this exercise, you will need to enlist the help of a friend, preferably someone that no one at your business would recognize. Now for the disguise. Nothing fancy or over the top like a clown wig, but something incognito. Maybe a hat and some sunglasses would be enough to keep your friend's cover.

Ask your friend to enter your business as a paying customer. The only thing they need to do is observe. If possible, ask them to record what they see with their phone, but only if they can be inconspicuous. Ask them to observe everything from the time they enter your business to the time they leave. If grabbing cell phone footage is not possible, ask them to take specific and detailed notes.

After the visit, ask for a detailed account of their interaction from beginning to end. If no one greeted them when they entered, you should know. If your employees were scrolling on their cell phones instead of paying attention to your customers, you should know. If your employees were sagging their pants, speaking inappropriately, or simply displaying a lousy attitude, you should know. The good thing is that all of these issues can be addressed and corrected, but the first step is seeing things from your customer's point of view and accepting the truth, no matter how jarring.

If you don't have a physical location, this exercise can still work. If you are the proprietor, have your friend call you and walk them through your entire process until the end of the transaction. Have them give you feedback about every step. Find out how they felt along the way and embrace the feedback with open arms. You may think you are doing everything right; however, your customers may not feel the same way. There is that old saying, if you stand in poop too long, after a while you won't be able to smell it. That same concept applies for your business. Sometimes we get so caught up in our own agendas and routines that we lose sight of some of the important details that matter.

As the business owner, you may perceive yourself as delivering stellar customer service, while your customers may perceive something very different. Now here is where you have to eat a big slice of humble pie and accept the fact that the only perception that matters is the customer's perception. If you can accept that, then you are one step closer to better customer service.

CHAPTER 15

All About Attitude

Your attitude is the cornerstone of your business. The attitudes of your employees are a direct reflection of *your* attitude. You set the tone of how customer service is conducted within your business. Your employees will always take their cue from you. As the leader of your business, it is your responsibility to set the standard and clearly define what behavior "is" and "is not" acceptable when it comes to the customer service your business provides. One of the most important attributes to have is a positive attitude. No matter how frustrating a situation may be, it is your job to remain calm and apply the service principles that you have developed for *your* business. Having a positive attitude means that you look to see the good in people, even when all they are giving you is the bad. Attitude drives the customer service engine that will ultimately drive you to a successful or an unsuccessful customer satisfaction rating.

I believe we all know—or at least think we know—what attitude means. According to Merriam-Webster, "attitude" is defined as a position assumed for a specific purpose. It is further defined as a feeling or emotion toward a fact or state. There are further definitions that explore the concept pertaining to having a negative or hostile state of mind, but we want to stay far away from those definitions. If we apply the first rendition of the definition, everything begins with your approach and overall position around customer service. Some people argue that the customer is always right, while others may strongly disagree. The reality is that there is truth to be had on both sides of the argument. In order to truly master the art of customer service and maintain a profitable business, one would have to become skilled at balancing both perspectives.

The phrase "the customer is always right" was popularized and pioneered by successful retailers Harry Gordon Selfridge, John Wanamaker and Marshall Field in the early 1900s. Their intention was to foster the novel idea of customer satisfaction in its most fundamental essence. They believed that business owners should take a customer's complaints seriously, making certain that the customer did not feel undervalued or defrauded, especially during a period where business owners maintained very cavalier attitudes toward ethics and customer satisfaction. During that time, most transactions were governed by the legal principle "caveat emptor".

"Caveat emptor" is a Latin phrase that means "let the buyer beware." It is a legal principle that places the responsibility on the *buyer* to make sure they are getting what they pay for and to be aware of any potential issues with a product or service *before* making a purchase. In other words, it is up to the buyer to be cautious and to do their own due-diligence before making a purchase.

The unconventional "customer is always right" philosophy portrayed a severely needed, well overdue, avant-garde attitude towards unethical customer service practices. This new attitude shifted some of the responsibility from the customer and forced the business owner to become somewhat liable for offering inferior products and services. While the customer still was required to conduct proper due diligence before entering into a transaction, this new ideology around customer satisfaction helped put consumers at ease and inspire them to buy with less worry. While the "customer is always right" approach changed the climate of customer service for the better, there was one caveat. There was no provision to address dishonest or entitled consumers.

With the evolution of more "responsible" customer service practices, there was always a propensity for unscrupulous consumers to exploit obvious loopholes. Most of the time, those overzealous "customer is always right" flag wavers usually intended to capitalize on this opportunity by defrauding vulnerable businesses for personal gain. While "the customer is always right" ethos was a catalyst for making sure that proper emphasis was put on making consumers the primary focus, it can be reasonably argued that it was not meant to be taken literally. It can be presumed that their overall goal was to make customers feel valued by training their staff to adopt a customer-centric approach where the customer is always treated as if they were right, irrespective of the situation.

While the concept was great in theory, it created a huge conflict that challenged the profitability of a business. At any given moment a business could potentially lose money while trying to uphold this new ideology. Fortunately, this new ideology did not encourage business owners to totally reverse their way of thinking, but instead to embrace new opportunities and try to find common ground with the consumer.

Over the years, "the customer is always right" philosophy has gradually evolved into a basic customer service tenant that embraces the idea of consumers being treated with respect and dignity, even if they are wrong. While the application of this tenet can be challenging, it truly reflects the changing attitudes of business owners. It has ultimately motivated them to change their priorities from being more business centric to being more customer centric.

One of the great seemingly true tall tales of a legendary customer service experience is the infamous story about Nordstrom (and yes you can Google it!). Allegedly, a man walked into a Nordstrom store with a tire, asking to return it for a refund. The salesperson was surprised, as Nordstrom does not sell tires. However, the salesperson decided to offer the man a refund anyway, as a gesture of goodwill and to maintain Nordstrom's reputation for excellent customer service. This story is often cited as an example of Nordstrom's commitment to its customers and their satisfaction. By going above and beyond what is expected, Nordstrom was able to create a positive customer experience that has become legendary.

So what is the moral of this story? Having a good attitude and applying a little common sense can go a long way in customer service! Had that employee had a bad attitude and had been adamant about not accepting the tire as a return, this ever so popular story would serve as the viral inspirational story that it is.

Now to address the elephant in the room. Did the customer really not know that he did not purchase the tire from Nordstrom? Maybe. Maybe not. We will honestly never know if he was intentionally being dishonest, but that doesn't really matter. What matters is that the salesperson (hopefully with permission) chose to accept a return of the tire which did cost the company a small financial loss, but the monetary setback was nominal compared to the intrinsic value that this great customer service story has delivered for Nordstrom.

The takeaway here is that no matter what the situation, your attitude and the attitude of your employees should always present in a way that makes the customer feel special. That does not necessarily mean that the customer is always right, but it does mean that you should be focused on finding the balance between creating a great customer experience and your business's bottom line. In order to achieve this, you need to ensure that your staff first has the right attitude and second, the mental fortitude to make sound, common sense decisions that won't destroy your company's reputation or send you to the poor house either. As I stated at the beginning of this chapter, everyone in your business will look to your attitude to set the tone. You need to truly believe that your customers are important enough to be given the benefit of the doubt. You also need to come to the realization that there will be some dishonest consumers that will challenge your policies and your position, all in the name of getting over. This is where you will need to maintain a professional and compassionate attitude, use common sense, and tap into that entrepreneurial intuition that has guided you thus far.

One tool that can be effective in helping you achieve this balance is the power of systems. A system is simply a set of methods, guidelines, and rules that are established to guide a particular process with a certain level of consistency and objectivity. How do you do that? I figured that you would ask! Let's move into the next chapters and find out.

CHAPTER 16

You Need Employees, Not Homies

One of the greatest benefits to being a black-owned business is having the ability to create jobs not only for people in the community, but for friends and family as well. There is, however, one caveat. Everyone is not a good fit to work in your business. Yes, I know this feels like a punch to the gut, but it's the truth. Sometimes you have to draw a hard line between business and friendship. Of course it may cause some friction during those weekend hangouts, but you need to understand that *your business* needs to be protected at all costs. If you establish ground rules from the beginning, you will save yourself from potential headaches down the road.

One of the first things you need to do is take inventory of the work that needs to be done in your business. Develop job titles with accurate job descriptions. Establish an employee guide that includes rules and expectations. Establish a hiring process. Use an objective set of eyes to help you with this process. Sometimes it's difficult to remove our personal feelings from the process, but in order to be successful, you will need to learn this skill or hire someone to manage the hiring process for you.

Another thing you have to consider is how other employees might perceive your relationship with your friends and family in the workplace. Do you show favoritism? Would you know if you were showing favoritism? Are you prepared to terminate your friend's employment if they were hurting your business? This is something that no one wants to think about and unfortunately, they end up losing an employee and a friend. One thing you have to remember is that every employee needs a basic understanding of what is and what is not acceptable when it comes to customer service in *your business*. In fact, you should have created, or be in the process of creating, some kind of standardized training for your staff. You can do it in person or you can invest in a web-based or video-based training. Take time and think about how you want your staff to approach customer service on behalf of your business.

Generally speaking, you want to make sure you have solid policies and procedures in place to help your staff navigate through situations when you may not be there. Of course, the people you hire should have a certain level of skill when it comes to dealing with the public. Would you really want your friend, that's known to be a live wire, handling customer issues on your behalf? I can literally see your money flying out the window right now! Let's face it, there are going to be times when customers push all of your buttons and get you almost to the point of a knuckle resolution; however, you must remember that you are a business owner, and this is just a part of business. Usually it's never personal, *unless* a customer has a personal vendetta against you.

Employees may find it difficult to separate conflict that occurs on business time. For some, the slightest confrontation can escalate into an unfortunate series of events that can tarnish your company's reputation long after that employee finds another job. The bottom line here is that you need to have a keen sense on whether a potential employee has what it takes to deliver the level of service that your business requires.

Using the A.C.I.E. criteria is a useful way to help you identify the distinguishing and foundational customer service traits of a potential new hire. A.C.I.E stands for Amiable, Conscientiousness, Intuitive, and Empathetic. These four characteristics are the pillars of a good customer service employee. Let's break them down.

Amiable

At a minimum, your potential employee should be pleasant and friendly. If you feel like you have to pull a smile or any sense of warmth out of a person during the interview, you should realize at this point that it may not get any better. Customer service begins at a person's core. The caliber of people you are looking to represent your business should have a naturally friendly personality. They should appear to be approachable. If you feel intimidated or uncomfortable talking to them during the interview, think about how your customers may feel interacting with them during a transaction.

Conscientiousness

Any potential employee will need to have an internal desire to follow through and complete tasks. This type of person will take ownership of a situation and will dedicate themselves to resolving an issue. People who are conscientiousness will most likely pay attention to detail, set goals, and work towards a plan to achieve those goals. Conscientious people are more likely to show up on time and work hard until the job is complete. Employees who are conscientious tend to be productive workers with a good work ethic.

Intuitive

After demonstrating the first two basic characteristics, your candidate should display some level of intuitiveness. We are not looking for someone to claim clairvoyance; however, they should be able to read the room. Your employees should be able to look for the signs and clues that a customer is unhappy before the customer makes a verbal complaint. They need to be able to look at a fidgeting customer waiting in line, address the wait time, and be able to acknowledge the wait time in a way that puts your customer at ease. Some of this skill will come with training, but a potential candidate should already have a good grasp of this ability.

Empathy

This may be the most important characteristic that a potential employee needs to possess in order to deliver authentic and deferential customer service. In my opinion, the ability to empathize is something that cannot be taught as part of a standalone training. A person needs to develop this skill over time. Life experiences, developmental opportunities, along with upstanding family values all are instances that help cultivate one's empathetic ability. Empathetic ability becomes ingrained within our DNA over time. I also believe that this special ability is divinely gifted to worthy individuals. Now here is where I defer to my affinity to the story of Jesus Christ. While this may not be part of your belief system, rest assured you can continue to read and take some value from the observations that I will present. In my opinion, Jesus Christ is the ultimate example of empathy. Empathy involves the capacity to place oneself in another's position. For God himself to enter into our world in the form of a man, suggests that even God knew the importance of experiencing humanity from within our frame of reference. The capacity and the ability to place oneself in another position is, in my opinion, ethereal. In order for one to possess the ability to achieve such a feat, I believe that God must have touched their lives in such a manner that inspired them to follow his blueprint, consciously or subconsciously. That is what makes this trait so amazing. It seems to have to be ordained by God and instilled within certainindividuals. If you are fortunate enough to come across a candidate with this innate quality, they may just be a blessing in disguise.

You should consider putting together a personal test for all of your potential new employees. You need to know their baseline skill and ability level. They should at least possess three of the traits outlined by A.C.I.E and potentially tracking towards the fourth. Aside from the abilities to actually do the job your business requires them to do, your potential new hires should possess these four basic foundational customer service traits if they are expected to have any encounters with your customers.

*See appendix a for sample interview questions

CHAPTER 17

Get on the Training Train

One of the major culprits behind poor customer service (aside from poor hiring choices), is the lack of proper training within an organization. There are many things that can be taught; however, without those four foundational characteristics, the chances for success are limited. As with anything, in order to build something great, you need to start with a solid foundation. When building your dream team of employees, you need to first make sure that the caliber of talent is top notch. There is no way that any pro sports team would go into a season with a team full of subpar players. In order for a team to be great, they must start with capable and competent people. They don't necessarily need to be completely polished, but their skill set should be suitable enough to help you elevate the level of your customer service.

So…assuming you have hired the right team of people, the next critical thing you need to focus on is training. Training. Training. And yes, more training! As the owner (and sometimes coach) of your team of star players, you will need to guide, teach, and condition your employees to be the best customer service team in the league. In order to achieve this, you must give them the tools they need to succeed and set levels of expectation and accountability. What happens when a player constantly drops the ball or continually misses a play that contributes to the team's loss? That player will most likely lose their position or ultimately be cut from the team. What happens when the team continues to lose? Ticket sales drop, merchandise sales decline, and the overall morale of the franchise is dispirited. The same kind of tribulations can affect your business if you allow your customer's experience to continually deteriorate into a series of lackluster transactions.

Unfortunately, modern society has indoctrinated the latter generations to subscribe to a fallible belief system which implies that simple participation deserves a reward. Strangely, this ideology has caused a severe degradation in work ethic and has sadly ushered in an era of mediocrity. Your business is your team franchise and you can't afford mediocrity. Professional sports teams invite individuals to become a part of their franchise because that individual demonstrates a natural ability and has the desire to play the game. Each individual's contribution makes the team stronger and vice versa. Each of your employees must demonstrate natural ability and desire. Natural ability can be nurtured through proper training while desire cannot. Desire is something that must be brought to the table.

If you haven't already, I strongly advise you to take a moment and assess your current team. When was the last time you did an employee evaluation? Are you satisfied with their current progress? Have you dropped the ball on the training? If you have, don't panic; there is still time to make a change…but don't wait too long!

CHAPTER 18

Customer Service and Sales

Customer service isn't just about finding a quick solution to any one customer problem. It's about fostering a trustworthy, long-term relationship, one where each customer interaction offers opportunities for deeper and more valuable engagement. Customer service is also an essential component of driving cross-sell and upsell opportunities. Providing a stellar customer service experience will help lay the foundation for cross selling and upselling opportunities.

Customer service and sales are closely related and should be treated as equal parts of the customer satisfaction equation. By providing a first-class customer service experience, businesses increase the likelihood that customers will spend more money buying additional products or services. It's one of those things where you want to work smarter and not harder. In order to capitalize on these opportunities, you will need to develop a strategy around your approach. Here are a few tips that can help you increase your business's propensity for cross-sell conversions.

Tip 1: Create a positive overall customer experience

When customers have positive customer service experiences with a business, they are more likely to become repeat customers, spend more money on additional products and services, and recommend your business to others. If you are able to wow your customers, you will not only win their trust and loyalty, you can also win more wallet share.

Tip 2: Build trust with your customers

Trust is one of the key factors that drives cross-sell opportunities. Customers who have confidence in a business are more inclined to buy additional products or services. Customers respond well to businesses that demonstrate a certain acumen in accountability. By being responsive, helpful, and empathetic, your customer service team can create a positive impact on your company's bottom line!

Tip 3: Identify your customer's needs

Another important aspect of leveraging customer service to help drive cross-sell opportunities is identifying your customer's needs. By truly understanding what your customer's problems or needs are, an attentive customer service team can recommend products or services that meet those needs or solves their specific problem. Your customer service team can play a critical role in this process by asking probing questions, listening to customer concerns, and capitalizing on opportunities to recommend additional products or services.

Tip 4: Train your staff to upsell and cross-sell

Upselling and cross-selling are two common techniques used to increase sales and drive additional revenue. Upselling involves recommending a higher-priced version of a product or service, while cross-selling involves recommending a related product or service. With upselling, a sales representative can potentially recommend a higher priced product or service, especially when that product or service will add value to a customer's well being and potentially solve one or more of their disclosed problems. With cross-selling, a sales representative may recommend a related product or service that complements the customer's purchase.

Tip 5: Follow up with your customers

Following up with customers after a purchase can also be an effective way to drive cross-sell opportunities. By reaching out to customers to ensure that they are satisfied with their purchase and to offer additional products or services, businesses can increase the likelihood of repeat purchases. Customer service representatives can play a critical role in this process by following up with customers after a purchase and making recommendations based on the customer's needs. For example, if a customer has purchased a product, the representative might follow up to ensure that the customer is satisfied and then offer additional products or services that complement the purchase.

As you can see, by training your employees properly, you can potentially develop a highly efficient sales team that can engage your customers in a way that will reflect in your bottom line.

Problem-solving is a huge part of providing a spectacular customer service experience. One of the most rewarding moments a business owner can have is the feeling generated when you are able to solve a problem for your customer. In most cases, that is your primary goal. Your products and services will ultimately provide a solution for your customers. A customer that achieves that feeling of confidence when using your product will most likely not only return as a repeat buyer, they may also show interest in buying more products. Solving problems equals making more money, and there is absolutely nothing wrong with that!

CHAPTER 19

The Cost of Bad Customer Service Part I

"It takes 20 years to build a reputation and five minutes to ruin it.
If you think about that you'll do things differently."

~ Warren Buffet

Some people may fail to see the connection between the customer experience and sales; however, this is a grave mistake and should be reevaluated if you fall into this category. According to NewVoice-Media's 2018 "Serial Switchers" report, businesses stand to lose more than $75 billion due to poor customer service. (2) That's right. It's a big number so let that sink in for a moment. Unfortunately, there is no data that I found that separates out black-owned businesses, but it doesn't really matter in this case because black-owned businesses are businesses... period. Black-owned businesses face the same customer service challenges that all other businesses face, except black-owned businesses are still impacted by "the black factor", which can exponentially and disproportionately affect their businesses.

When a big box brand store like Walmart or Target loses one retail customer, the impact is very insignificant and may not raise any red flags; however, if a small black-owned mom and pop retail store loses one good customer, they may almost certainly feel the impact. The worst thing that can happen to a business is watching their dollars walk out the front door.

Why does money walk out of the door? A business will typically lose customers for the following reasons:

1. Inferior products or services
2. Non-competitive pricing
3. Poor customer service

Now there are some brainiac gurus out there that will have a slew of in-depth statistics and reports showing a hundred other additional arguments on why businesses lose customers, and respectively they may have some valid useful points; however, since we are primarily focusing on black-owned small businesses, I think the most prudent approach is to focus on the three most prominent factors. With that being said, because the topic of this book is dealing with customer service, we will focus on the latter.

According to Zendesk's CX Trends Report for 2023, 73% of consumers say they would switch to a company's competitor after just one bad customer service experience. (3) Holy cow! That means that you have about a 75% chance of losing one customer if you provide bad service only once! If we drill down further and focus only on African American consumers, I am almost certain that the number of consumers that switch to a competitor after only one bad encounter will increase exponentially. This figure is of course affected by…you got it, "the black factor".

Here's where it should get real for you. How many customers do you service on a daily basis? How many on a weekly basis? How many on a monthly basis? Do you see where this is going? How many customers can you afford to lose?

You may think that losing one customer is not a big deal; however, when you look at the cost to acquire a new customer versus the cost to retain a customer, you may want to reconsider your strategy. Statistics have shown that it may cost more than 5 times more to acquire a customer than to keep an existing one (we will talk more about this in the next chapter). When you consider all the costs for marketing, promotion and let's not forget the time you spend courting your customers, answering questions and convincing them to buy—it all adds up. Just think about all of the hard work and money that you have invested into selling your product to that one customer, only to have it all slip away because of one avoidable customer service blunder. In short, retaining and cross selling to your existing customers is much more cost-effective than finding and onboarding new customers.

As you can see, it is almost impossible to separate sales from service. Considering one without the other is shortsighted and your business will suffer. In my experience, I have worked for Fortune 500 companies and have witnessed firsthand the separatists approach to sales and service. The sales team would be driven by high sales goals with little to no responsibility for customer service. There was, however, a customer sales team, and all customer services issues were funneled to that team. From onboarding to service issues, it was the customer service team's responsibility to handle all of these calls. Of course this all sounded good, especially to the sales team whose focus were primarily sales pipelines and bonus payouts. Being a member of the sales team myself, I could certainly appreciate the intentional focus on sales without the distraction of actually servicing clients. However, now as a business owner and as a person that has a vested interest in seeing black-owned businesses overcome their customer service challenges, I can appreciate the duality of sales and service.

Actually, in hindsight, I must admit that I did at times feel the repercussions of separating service and sales while in those types of sales positions. Spending time building relationships with prospects and customers, only to turn them over to another group of people just didn't seem right. After making a sale and almost immediately needing to herd them off to another person for service felt cold. I could feel myself being pulled away from the customer. Sometimes I felt like I was in a scene from a Spike Lee joint—you know, the iconic scenes where the person is the only thing moving on screen. The sad reality is…most customers felt the same way, except they were moving in the opposite direction away from me, the person whom which they'd built a relationship with.

I am certain that the company had its own rationale for setting up their sales and service departments in such a way, but after a few more years of experience and developing an affinity for good customer service, I now am realizing how wrong that process was. The truth is, everyone has an active role in customer service—or shall I say, the "customer experience".

In order to provide a truly exceptional customer experience, you have to take a holistic approach. The reality is, there is no such thing as a "standalone" customer service department. Everyone is the customer service department. A business becomes counterproductive when they prevent the opportunity of sales and service from working in tandem with one another. Furthermore, it can feel like you are pouring water into a bottomless glass if you are losing existing customers just as fast as you are bringing them in. While onboarding new customers is necessary for growth, it is absolutely critical that you pay attention to your existing customers. Neglecting customers that already see the value in what you are offering can be a huge costly mistake. In the next chapter, we will take a closer look at the negative financial ramifications that occur when the customer experience goes bust.

CHAPTER 20

The Cost of Bad Customer Service Part 2

Providing excellent customer service is not only important for building customer loyalty and brand reputation, it can also have a direct impact on your company's bottom line. When customers have a bad customer service experience, they are less likely to purchase products or services from that company which can ultimately lead to significant financial losses.

When a customer has a bad experience, they are more likely to churn. Customer churn, also known as customer attrition, is the rate at which customers stop doing business with a company for any reason during a specified period of time.

Some amount of customer churn is to be expected and is a natural part of the business cycle. You will learn (if you haven't already) that you will inevitably lose customers from time to time for various reasons, often for causes outside of your control. Customers move away, their needs change, or they may just get a better offer somewhere else. It's going to happen; however, if you are seeing a high churn rate in your customer base, then you have a problem that requires your immediate attention. The increasing loss of loyal customers indicates that you potentially may have issues with your products, your service, or it could be an indicator that your customer service delivery is lacking. If your customers are leaving before you've recouped their onboarding costs, you're losing money. You no longer can depend on that revenue from that customer, and it also means that you've squandered away the time and money you've spent on marketing and advertising to bring them in.

So...what is a good customer churn rate? Of course, there is no single correct number. Churn rates vary depending on your business model and the industry that you are in, but there are some guidelines which you can use to help you determine where you stand.

Without scouring the internet for detailed reports on every industry's churn rate, I would safely assume that the average among most industries is 2-10%.In most industries, a 2-10% churn rate is good, or at least acceptable. To calculate churn rate, you simply follow a few steps and conduct a few calculations using a simple formula.

In order to begin the calculation, you need to know the total number of customers that you lost and the number of lost customers at the start of the period. These two numbers help establish the churn rate. Now all you have to do is follow the steps below and prepare to become horrified by your alarmingly high customer churn rate. Okay, maybe it won't be that bad. Hopefully it won't be that bad, but whether good, bad, or ugly, you need to embrace the number and begin an action plan to get things back on track, or improve upon what you are doing right.

Now, follow the steps below to figure out what your customer churn number is.

1. Choose a time period. You can choose to evaluate it on a week, month, quarter or annual basis. I would suggest focusing on calculating this number on a monthly basis; that way, you can stop the bleeding if you are noticing consistent losses.
2. Determine the number of customers you had at the beginning of that time period.
3. Determine the number of customers you had lost at the end of that time period.
4. Divide the number of lost customers by the number of customers

you had prior to the attrition.
5. Multiply that number by 100.

Here is what the simple formula looks like assuming you are calculating your monthly churn rate.

(Number of Lost Customers at the end of the month / Total Customers at the Start of Time Period) × 100 = Churn Rate

Let's take a look at an example.

Suppose in the beginning of December, you know that you have 25 loyal customers. (Hopefully you are keeping records whether it be with a CRM or possibly some accounting software, but this is a number that you absolutely must keep track of. If you are not, then you need to start immediately!)

At the end of the month, you notice that you only have 19 customers. Here is the calculation:

Number of Lost Customers at the end of the month (6) / Total Customers at the Start of Time Period (25) = .24

.24 x 100 = 24% Churn Rate

In this example you would have calculated a 24% churn rate for the month of December. While a 24% attrition rate is a bit on the high side, you should always be tracking and comparing this number on a month to month basis. This will help you rule out any situational anomalies and give you an opportunity to drill down and find out where the issues lie. Researching and understanding the average churn rate within your market helps you gauge your performance and identify areas for improvement. As a simple rule of thumb, churn rates exceeding 15%

indicate potential issues with customer service performance and can serve as a general guideline. However, it's important to note that churn rates can vary significantly across industries and even among different business models within the same industry. Some industries naturally have higher churn rates due to various factors; therefore, it is crucial to consider industry-specific benchmarks while interpreting your own churn rate.

To determine the underlying reasons for high churn and assess customer satisfaction, you may want to consider conducting surveys and relying on social listening to obtain that insight. Your customers will almost always give you a truthful and honest explanation on why they no longer patronize your business. These communications can come directly from the customer in the form of customer surveys or it may come indirectly from online reviews. You should be actively monitoring social media platforms and review sites for any intel regarding feedback and overall sentiment surrounding your brand and customer satisfaction ratings. This information can guide you in making targeted improvements to your customer service, enhancing the overall customer experience, and reducing customer attrition.

As a black business owner, this information may be new to you; however, it behooves you to get up to speed quickly and use this information as a tool to help keep revenue flowing in and not out. For smaller businesses, this process may be a little bit easier because there is a smaller pool of customers to manage and keep track of, but as you grow, this should be a regular practice that grows with you.

CHAPTER 21

Expectation vs Excuses

Those of you, like myself, who have had the fortunate opportunity to work in customer service, will most likely have developed a certain tolerance when it comes to customer service snafus. It is because most of us, having experienced the unyielding wrath of an unhappy customer, are able to empathize with workers in most cases. Even if you have not had the pleasure of being berated by a distressed patron, you hopefully have been blessed with the rare gift of patience and understanding. I would argue that most people under most circumstances have the capacity to be understanding, or shall I even dare to say... forgiving. I might even go out on a limb to say most people are willing to accept certain customer service failures within reason, given that they are still treated with respect and greeted with honesty.

One of the best things you can do for your customers when something goes awry is to offer them some kind of thoughtful mediation. Take ownership of the situation and make them feel confident that you will resolve their issue in a way that makes them feel whole. The worst thing you can do is offer up excuses and point fingers. At the end of the day, no matter who did or didn't do something, the responsibility rests squarely on your shoulders. Don't insult your customers by playing the blame game.

If you own a beauty salon and you overbook a few appointments for the day, is it right to expect your customers to wait and suffer for your mistake? If you own a contracting company, is it acceptable to miss a scheduled customer appointment because you couldn't find a babysitter? Hopefully, you don't share this information with your customer because at face value, it will unequivocally sound like an excuse, but on a deeper level, it displays a certain level of unprofessionalism.

Your customers are not paying you to hear your life story. They may be cordial and all smiles as you tell your tale of woe, but just know in the back of their mind they are already thinking of a viable replacement for you.

So, how can you come out a winner in this situation? The best approach is to set reasonable and realistic expectations in the most professional possible manner. Instead of telling your customer that you need to reschedule their appointment because you are having babysitting issues, try this approach. Explain to your customer there was an unexpected conflict that requires you to reschedule their appointment at another time that is convenient to them. You should also offer them a discount or throw in some kind of compensating reward for their trouble. Doesn't this sound better than "I can't make it because I don't have a babysitter."?

Making excuses for customer service inadequacies creates an atmosphere of defensiveness rather than resolution. Failure to take ownership of issues can frustrate customers and strain your relationship. On the other hand, setting proper expectations demonstrates transparency and a willingness to proactively resolve an issue before the customer realizes there is one. By being upfront about limitations or constraints, you can prevent potential disappointments and work towards feasible solutions without looking disreputable. Be sure to provide clear and frequent communication so that your customer will have a clear understanding of what to expect during the resolution process.

This approach encourages customers to have confidence in your ability to satisfy their needs and address their concerns in a prompt and professional manner. Far too many times black-owned businesses make the mistake of becoming too "chummy" with their customers simply because of a shared ethnicity. This may not apply to all situations, but I am specifically addressing this point because black consumers are typically the ones calling foul when black-owned businesses fall short.

Managing customer expectations is a skill that takes time to develop; however, you should be able to grasp the fundamentals discussed in this chapter quickly. If you haven't already begun thinking about it, you should begin anticipating potential issues and developing potential solutions. Remember, your execution will fail if your preparation is lacking.

CHAPTER 22

All EARS

In order to be effective, you have to be all ears. It all begins with listening, but aside from that, I am talking about the acronym EARS. This is something that I have developed for use in my own business. Of course, there are tons of clever acronyms used to guide you through different customer service situations. If you search Google, I am sure that you will have days of material to read through. As a business owner, I wanted to put my own clever spin on the tools that I used for my customer service process. I developed the concept of E.A.R.S. You have to be all ears. It's not reinventing the wheel, but it's a technique that I specifically tailored for my use, and I encourage you to create some clever techniques of your own.

E.A.R.S simply means Empathize. Apologize. Repeat. Solve. It's basic yet effective. There are many other different acronyms with more steps and more complicated pieces, but keeping it simple is key. If the customer already has a problem, why drag them through a long roadmap of insincere rehearsed punishment? Let's take a deeper dive into each of these steps.

Empathize

What is empathy? Merriam-Webster dictionary defines "empathy" as the action of understanding, being aware of, being sensitive to, and vicariously experiencing the feelings, thoughts and experience of another without necessarily having those feelings. So in order to empathize with your customers, you must put yourself in their shoes. You must acknowledge that what they are feeling is real, even though you may not have experienced their pain. For example, if you serve someone coffee with pure sugar and they asked for stevia extract, they most certainly have a grievance. To most people it may not be a big deal, but what if the customer is a diabetic? It's not up to you to decide the importance of their grievance. It's your job to listen, acknowledge, and substantiate their concerns.

Empathy statements can also be useful in conflict resolution, as they provide a way to see the situation from another person's perspective. By using empathy statements, we can learn to connect with others on a deeper level and create a more benevolent customer experience.

Apologize

The next step is to apologize, but before you do, you need to learn how to apologize. Admitting fault is a slippery slope and if you say the wrong thing you could wind up with a lawsuit. Although some irate customers may threaten legal action, they most likely will not pursue that option, especially if they feel that you are genuinely trying to remedy their issue. The best way to apologize is to express a sincere regret that their experience was not the best.

Repeat

When a customer is venting, the best thing to do is to let them finish. Once they are done, repeat what they have just told you. It doesn't have to be verbatim, but you need to make sure that you have included all of the details. Take notes while listening if you have to. Repeating the customer's concerns back to them does two things.

1. It confirms that you have heard all of their concerns correctly.
2. It validates your interest in helping resolve their issue.

A good way to begin the conversation at this stage is to start by saying something like this...

"Let me make sure that I understand all of your concerns correctly..."

Solve

Solving the customer's problem is the end goal. When you are able to solve a customer's problem, you become the hero. Unfortunately, there are some instances where you simply will not be able to solve a customer's problem in that moment; however, you still need to work towards a resolution. The one thing you cannot do is offer your customer excuses. Customers look for solutions, not excuses. They are not interested in "pass the buck blame" games. Even if their issue was not created by you, you need to reassure the customer that you are making your best efforts to make them whole.

All of your employees need to be trained and have a mastery of this process. Your employees need to understand that solving customer issues is non-negotiable and is expected as part of their employment. There have been times when I have actually heard an employee tell a customer, "That's not my department," then walks off leaving the customer standing there. As a matter of fact, I've been told the exact same phrase just before being abandoned by an employee. Do you want to guess what I did? You probably guessed it…I abandoned my shopping cart and went to another store. The simple concept of E.A.R.S can help you establish a consistent process when dealing with customer situations.

CHAPTER 23

How to Say No

In some instances, it may be necessary to inform a client that you cannot provide a specific product or service. However, there is something about the words "no" or "can't" that really rub people the wrong way. In fact, I'm strongly inclined to believe that when a customer hears the word "no" or "can't", it is immediately translated into "won't." How can I be sure of this? Because I'm guilty of it. We all are, whether knowingly or subconsciously; we all have a built-in skepticism that activates when we feel like someone is "out to get us." When an African American customer walks into a black-owned business, it is absolutely imperative that you do everything in your power to diffuse their pessimism from the start; otherwise, anything that you say or do could backfire and make you the latest subject of the black-owned business blues.

There undoubtedly will be times when you will need to say no to a client; it's a part of business just as it is a part of life, but as with anything, it's all about how you position and deliver your response. When a customer is already upset, you have to take special care not to agitate the situation by being callous and insensitive. This can sometimes mean leaning into a bit of psychology in your approach. I would argue that most of the time, customers can be understanding if they are given the opportunity to be. In many cases, customer service situations spiral out of control because businesses often take a hardline approach with little to no consideration of the customer's feelings. Yes, I said feelings. After all, in order for a customer to have a great customer experience, they have to feel it, which means emotion is often a driving factor.

Being told no by someone whom you supposedly view as an ally can be a devastating blow to one's pride. It's insulting. It's antagonizing. It's embarrassing. It's everything that you do not want your customer to feel. That is why it is extremely important to avoid using negative impact words such as "no" and "can't". Instead, take a moment and make sure that you truly understand what your customer is trying to accomplish with their transaction. By having a clear understanding of their needs, you will be able to redirect them to alternative options that may help them solve their problem. Here are some additional tips to consider.

Tip 1: Offer alternative solutions.

Whether saying no with a smile or with a grimace, you run the risk of providing an unfavorable customer experience. The truth is, there are times that we have to say no, but there is an underrated skill of being able to say no without saying no. I know. It sounds a little confusing, but in fact it's very simple. You have to be able to train your mind into believing that "no" does not exist. "No" is simply a construct in which inadequacy exists. It could be that one has inadequate resources to complete a task. It could be that one has inadequate information to make a decision. According to the Merriam-Webster dictionary, "No" is used as a function word to express the negative of an alternative choice or possibility. Following this logic, it is your responsibility to provide the customer with the possibility of alternate choices.

Instead of saying no, try offering similar options that can potentially solve their problem. Remember, the primary focus is to solve the customer's problem. Try keeping the conversation focused on what you can do instead of what you can't do. By keeping their attention focused on the shiny object in your right hand, they will most likely forget that there is nothing in your left hand.

Tip 2: Be upfront and honest about your limitations.

You may have heard an old saying that goes "jack of all trades, master of none." I reference this old quote to emphasize the fact that everyone cannot be good at everything all of the time. There are some things that you will be able to do better than others and you need to relay that to your customers and set realistic expectations from the start.

By providing a clear and concise explanation of any restrictions or constraints that may prevent you from fulfilling a customer's request, you can potentially avert that customer's disappointment, help them re-adjust their expectations, and deliver a satisfying customer service experience by helping them find resolution to their problem. This approach can help the customer understand the situation without feeling outright denied, while giving them the opportunity to evaluate other suitable options.

Tip 3: Lean into your company's policies.

Remember a few chapters back where I mentioned systems and processes? This is where those systems can potentially save your bacon. If you have established specific policies or guidelines that prevent you from fulfilling a customer's request (and hopefully you have!), feel free to respectfully refer to them in those less than ideal situations. These systems help you to position your decision as a result of established rules rather than a personal refusal. These policies should be ingrained in all of your employee's minds, universally employed and enforced, and communicated in an open and honest fashion. By demonstrating that you are adhering to an equitable and impartial set of standards and policies, it lessens the likelihood of that customer feeling singled out and treated differently than everyone else.

Tip 4: Be understanding and show empathy.

If you haven't noticed by now, empathy has been an underlying theme throughout this book. Why? Because it demonstrates a deliberate and deeper understanding of how a customer is actually feeling. True empathy comes from a sincere desire to understand what your customer is experiencing. Empathy should not be misconstrued as empty robotic rhetoric spewed at the first sign of customer opposition. Empathy is the most pragmatic way to soften the impact of a negative response.

Again the takeaway here is to remember that finding a solution for your customer is the primary objective, even when you have to deliver a negative response. With that being said, there will be some occasions where no means no…period. These instances are usually limited to situations where someone is asking you to do something illegal or unethical. In these cases, you absolutely need to stand on your principles and unequivocally inform those individuals that you will in no way honor those types of requests. Remember, protecting your brand should always be a priority.

CHAPTER 24

Understanding Emotional Triggers

We live in a sensitive society. Over the years, people are more easily offended by a number of different triggers stemming from different circumstances in their own lives. Some could argue that people have become overly sensitized while others may argue that it's society who is not sensitive enough. No matter what side of the argument you choose to stand on, as a business owner, you most likely will need to understand and interact with triggered customers.

According to Merriam-Webster, the word "trigger" means to cause an intense and usually negative emotional reaction in someone. Healthline.com defines a trigger as anything that might cause a person to recall a traumatic experience. To put things in perspective, specifically from an African American point of view, the historical struggles faced by African Americans, such as slavery, segregation, and persistent systemic racism, can deeply affect their mental, emotional health and wellbeing.

In American society, businesses often stumble into customer interactions that may unintentionally (or intentionally) trigger or evoke underlying racial biases. The expressive and animated communication styles commonly observed in African American culture can sometimes be misinterpreted or misunderstood by individuals from diverse cultural backgrounds. Such misinterpretations can result in miscommunication, confusion, or even unintentional offense. The expectation in the African American community implicitly requires black-owned businesses to understand and embrace our passionate dispositions and sometimes overly animated personalities; however, oftentimes black-owned businesses sometimes approach customer interactions from a position of indifference. They operate on the supposition that any one of color should be happy and eager to hand their money over even if the service is lacking.

The audacity of expectation emerges from both the customer and the business owner's point of view. Instead of becoming a powerful cohesive economic force, we tend to often display irreconcilable behaviors that ultimately cause cash flow throughout the black community to become stagnant. Although the buyer and the seller share the responsibility to build economic stability within the black community, the onus is on the business owner to circumvent those triggering behaviors that can provoke those disparaging feelings within their African American consumers.

For some customers, past traumatic experiences related to customer service or personal triggers can be activated by bad customer service encounters. It could be reminiscent of previous negative experiences or trigger anxiety associated with unresolved conflicts or mistreatment. These emotions can resurface and impact the customer's emotional state.

So, here is the big question…why should this matter to you? I'm so glad that you asked! Here are some examples that should help bring the pieces of this puzzle together.

Let's assume you have a customer that has an issue and begins to express their complaint to one of your employees. Your employee, instead of helping them, becomes combative. Instead of listening, your employee cuts off every other word in an attempt to arrive at the destination of "I can't help you." Little does your employee know that this customer had been experiencing the same difficulty with her supervisor at work for the past year and a half. The same abrasive and dismissive tone. The blatant disrespect. Your employee's behavior reminds them of their supervisor, whom they despise. All of those feelings of disrespect and disregard have resurfaced in that very moment. How is the customer feeling now?

What is that customer thinking now? I'm pretty sure the answer is obvious, but let me paint another picture with another example.

Imagine that one of your customers is wandering aimlessly around your store, confused or obviously in need of assistance. They come across one of your employees and ask for help. Your employee tells the customer that they have to find the correct person to help, but never returns. What that employee doesn't know is that this customer has been dealing with the childhood trauma of being abandoned by their parents. This customer was always left by themselves at home for long periods of time not knowing when their parents would return. They had been faced with years or broken promises, waiting with a hopeless anticipation. Fast forward to now. In this moment, your employee's abandonment just made all of those emotions resurface. How do you think the customer feels now?

These two scenarios may be an over exaggeration, but they are very real delineations of real-life situations from a customer's perspective. Emotional triggers are very real and sometimes unavoidable. We all carry some level of unresolved emotional baggage around with us. It's a part of life. If you are going to empower your customer service team, this is something that you will need to embrace, learn, and teach to your team.

Of course, the overall goal is to avoid triggering your customers, but we have to be honest, that is something that is not always in our control. A customer can be potentially triggered before they even enter your store. They could have had a run in with a parking attendant. Someone could have stepped on their shoe without apologizing; the point is, you never know. Good customer service people are observant and should be able to recognize a potentially triggered consumer. At this point, your goal is to avoid exacerbating the situation. How do you do that? For starters, your customer service protocols should have already set the tone for a great customer service experience.

Next, focus on specific behaviors that can potentially de-escalate any tension. You have to remember, not only is their discontent tied to an emotional trigger, it is also tied to their wallets and their pocketbooks.

In the next section we are going to examine some potential triggers and discuss some tools that can help you and your team handle these issues and come out winners.

Non-Verbal Triggers

The best way to avoid tense encounters is to learn how to avoid certain triggers. There are many non-verbal cues that can often trigger a customer unintentionally. Let's be honest. Your employees often are working under pressure due to long shifts, servicing long lines, and dealing with disgruntled customers. Because of this, it is reasonable to expect your employees to succumb to some of the pitfalls that arise in the form of non-verbal triggers. These triggers can come in the form of nonverbal transactions, inadvertently manufactured from their own stress level. However, if your employees are properly trained and possess an adequate ability to somewhat navigate their emotions, they should be able to provide the required standard level of customer service with limited issues. Here are a few non-verbal triggers that you should absolutely avoid.

Attitude

We discussed the topic of attitude previously in Chapter 15, but understanding the role of one's attitude in relation to it being a non-verbal trigger is important. Before one word is spoken, a person's attitude should be communicated through a warm smile, direct eye contact, and an inviting posture. When customers encounter unhelpful or rude service providers, it can lead to frustration and anger. Poor communication, dismissive attitudes, or unresolved issues can trigger a sense of being disrespected or undervalued, causing customers to become emotionally upset and irate.

Body Language

Body language is also a major culprit. It's very easy for an employee to become frustrated when they are having a rough time; after all, we are all human. However, we have to train ourselves to push past those stressful hurdles and focus on the customer. After all, without those customers, none of us would have jobs!

There used to be a popular phrase used by a popular deodorant brand that said "never let them see you sweat." This is a skill that has to be developed. The first step is to tell yourself that nothing is personal—at least for you it shouldn't be. Most of the time, a customer's issue is situational and if handled incorrectly, becomes emotional. You have to be very cautious to pay attention to your own body language. Your posture speaks volumes. Keeping your arms folded or slouching displays dismissal and disrespect.

Frowning, scowling, or eye-rolling are sure indicators that someone is disgruntled. Sighing or heavy breathing also sets a negative tone. This behavior is not only juvenile, it's unprofessional, yet there have been times that I have suffered the occasional eye roll simply because I asked someone to do their job. Eye rolling is not acceptable in any situation; in fact, it can be considered passive aggressive behavior, which does not and should not align with acceptable customer service standards. Without saying a single word, you have already told your customer that they are bothering you.

Non-Urgency

Have you ever heard the phrase, "time is money"? When you or your staff waste a customer's time, you potentially lose the opportunity to win their money. Wasting a customer's time comes in many forms: from moving slow while ringing up their order to dragging your feet while looking for a manager to resolve a problem. As a customer, I don't appreciate when someone doesn't value my time. Slothfulness is a sure sign of disengagement and disrespect. It also tells your customer that your staff is not interested in helping them spend their money with you. In situations where customers are dealing with urgent matters, such as time-sensitive requests or critical problems, bad customer service can exacerbate their anxiety and stress levels. Delays, unhelpful responses, or inadequate solutions can intensify the pressure and trigger heightened emotional distress.

Inconsistency

There is nothing worse than a customer feeling like they are not getting the same standard of service as the next person, especially if they are spending their money at your business just the same. Each person patronizing your business should receive the exact same good customer service. Imagine standing behind a person in line and the cashier is really chummy with the person in front of you, and then when it's your turn at the register that same employee almost goes out of their way to give you the cold shoulder. How would that make you feel?

While you cannot control a person's perspective, you can control the narrative in which service is presented by your business. Your narrative should always be guided to make sure that every one of your customers and potential customers are presented with the same quality customer service experience every time.

Customers rely on service providers to offer expertise, guidance, and reassurance. When faced with unprofessional or incompetent customer service, customers may feel uncertain about the accuracy or reliability of the information provided. This can lead to feelings of insecurity, doubt, and skepticism towards the business or the products/services being offered.

Avoidance

Avoidance occurs when you or your staff actively evade customers. Typically this occurs when someone is looking to avoid the possibility of having to be accountable. This type of behavior happens when staff is lazy, lacks a serious work ethic, or simply does not take customer service serious. Have you ever wandered around a store looking for assistance, only to find that everyone has magically disappeared? Have you ever needed assistance and noticed a seemingly available person clutching onto a clipboard like what they are doing is more important than helping you spend your money in their establishment? Have you ever tried to get someone's attention and they intentionally avoid eye contact so they don't have to acknowledge you?

Creating an uncomfortable barrier by physically turning away to avoid customer interaction is an easy way to trigger your customer and usher money right out the door. Customers expect their concerns to be acknowledged and addressed promptly. However, when they experience unresponsive or indifferent customer service, it can evoke feelings of being disregarded or ignored. This lack of attention to their needs can generate emotions such as disappointment, frustration, or even a sense of insignificance.

Inattentiveness

Distracted behavior, such as checking phones, stocking displays, or even chatting with co-workers are all examples of disengagement. Disengagement indicates a lack of interest, or a deliberate decision to separate oneself from a particular situation. Inattentiveness in customer service can negatively impact the customer's experience, leading to the potential loss of business. Customers expect their concerns to be acknowledged and addressed promptly. However, when they experience unresponsive or indifferent customer service, it can evoke feelings of being disregarded or ignored. This lack of attention to their needs can generate emotions such as disappointment, frustration, or even a sense of insignificance.

Confrontational Behavior

Aggressive behavior creates a hostile and confrontational environment, which will undoubtedly make your customers feel uncomfortable, disrespected, or even threatened. It can escalate conflicts and potentially trigger fight or flight mentality within your customer. This type of escalation must be avoided at all costs. These types of aggressive behaviors include angry or aggressive gestures such as pushing, grabbing, snatching or slamming items, or even invading personal space. All of these may be understandable, but should never be acceptable under any circumstance.

I know we spent a lot of time discussing emotional triggers. Now let's take a walk on the other side...understanding triggers that affect business owners!

CHAPTER 25

A Business Owner Has Triggers Too!

So, we talked about potential customer triggers, but what about the business owner and their triggers? As you know, there are two sides to every coin. Just as your customers may deal with triggering events during their customer experience, business owners are not exempt from emotional trauma that may impact their behavior towards their customers. The reality is, you're more than a business owner. You're human. No one is exempt from emotional baggage; however, as a business owner, you have to learn how to compartmentalize your feelings and rely more on the systems that you set up for your business.

So what does this exactly mean? It means that you will need to take inventory of your emotional baggage. You have to ask yourself the following questions:

- What makes you angry and why?
- What words and actions do you think are disrespectful and why?
- What childhood experiences or past traumas might still affect you today?
- How do you typically react in stressful situations?
- What situations or behaviors consistently make you feel upset or uncomfortable?

These questions are designed to encourage introspection and help you gain a deeper understanding of your own potential emotional triggers. Identifying triggers is a crucial step in managing emotional reactions and promoting overall well-being. Keep in mind that some of your triggers may be rooted in unresolved issues or past experiences that continue to impact your emotions.

Now it's time to grab a pad and pen. Draw two columns. Write the answers to those questions in the left column. For example, if someone calling you an offensive name triggers you, write it down. If your parents always put you down and made you feel insignificant and worthless, write it down. Write it all down, then get prepared for the next step.

I'd like to think that in navigating through a business owner's triggers, this is a three-step process. Knowing and understanding your own triggers is only the first step. The second step requires one to go beyond the point of introspection and attempt to connect the dots. In this second step, you should write down the answers to all of your questions in one column. Study them. Analyze them, then think about how they may relate to your business. Think about the past few customer service transactions that went awry and could have possibly triggered you to some degree. What did the customer do or didn't do to trigger you? What did the customer say? Did they yell? Did they curse at you? Did they speak to you in a condescending manner?

Write all of your answers in the other column. Be honest. Take your time. These first two steps are critical.

Now that you have your two columns completed, let's put two and two together. This step is as simple as matchmaking. Draw a line from the bad customer service incident to the triggering life experience. Keep in mind that multiple incidents may track back to a single trigger. For example, if your last customer encounter resulted in the customer screaming at you, then you would draw a line to the corresponding trigger. This trigger could come from childhood trauma, or maybe from a previous job or other relationship where you were the victim of verbal abuse. Do you see where this is going? Do you see the connection? Good. This process plays a crucial part in understanding how to manage your triggers so that they do not influence damaging behaviors that may cause bad customer service experiences for your customers.

Now that you have a better understanding of what your triggers are and how they affect you, now comes the third step in this process. The action plan. This is where you think of ways to circumvent your triggers. This can be as simple as relying on your highly trained customer service manager to diffuse those problematic situations, or it can be as involved as you seeking professional counseling or therapy to help you navigate your issues in a more curative manner. The first thing you need to do in this step is to be honest with yourself. Some people are simply not wired to be a people person and this may have nothing to do with triggers. Some people are highly introverted. You have to take an honest assessment of your people skills. Do you cringe at the thought of confrontation? Do you have issues with setting boundaries? If the answers to these types of questions are yes, then you may have to accept the fact that you may not be the best person to handle the face-to-face customer service issues for your business. But don't worry, that is perfectly okay. Remember, people skills can be developed. Personalities can evolve. Triggers caused by traumatic life events can eventually heal; however, you will need to be willing to put in the work.

In order to navigate through your personal triggers,
you will need to humble yourself for the sake of your business.

You have to adopt and ingrain certain principles that allow you to separate your personal emotions from business affairs. You have to realize that every customer situation should not result in a fight or flight response. Although this can be an advantageous approach in life or death situations, most customer service interactions should not require you to default to "survival mode." If this is how you feel whenever a customer approaches, then you may have an anxiety or stress disorder that may ultimately require you to seek professional help to overcome this challenge.

Having control over your emotions will always give you an advantage in any customer service interaction. Believe it or not, some customers thrive off of instigation and manipulation in order to get what they want, and you will need to be able to ignore all of their agitation and stay focused on resolving their issue calmly.

Okay, so here is where we hit some bumpy terrain. All of the information up until this point is useful for everyone, but here is where I need to specifically address black business owners. If you can recall a few chapters back, I spoke about something that I call the black factor. If we are truly discussing triggers and emotions, then we cannot honestly attempt to solve this problem without including the black factor in the equation. Historically, culturally, and economically, black people have a history of pain, suffering and indifference. That is a fact. However, we can no longer allow that baggage to weigh us down during our journey. Should we forget about it? Absolutely not. It would be an injustice to forget. One thing we cannot do is use it as an excuse to punch people in the face at the first hint of disrespect. This may seem like an extreme example, but unfortunately it does happen. This also feeds into the stereotype of the angry black man and the angry black woman cliché. Unfortunately, as this country tries to rewrite or erase factual American history, they are also trying to diminish the atrocities committed towards black people in this country. Those atrocities most definitely contribute to the emotional triggers of the black community.

Those disparate and overtly discriminatory practices often shape the mindset of black business owners and black consumers. Because we have to learn to cope with so many triggers as a consumer and as a business owner, we are perpetually always in a state of fight or flight. Our default instinct is always survival mode. For some, survival mode translates into aggression. With this type of traumatic history, it's almost impossible to suppress those emotions attached with those triggers, but here is the caveat. Despite all of the historical hardship and adversity, as black business owners we must absolutely learn to recognize those triggers and train ourselves in the skilled art of restraint and redirection.

So how do I know all of this? Great question. From years of experience from all perspectives. As a consumer, I've been treated less than cordial. As an employee, I've been lied on by clients so that they could have their accounts transferred to my non-black counterparts. I've been called the N-word and threatened with physical violence. Now, as a business owner, I've faced subtle discrimination just by showing up as a black proprietor. But I also have to be brutally honest. As a business owner, I can't really say that I am triggered emotionally by much of the stigma that comes with bigotry. In fact, the main thing that triggers me as a business owner is when someone does not value my time, and that comes in many forms. For me, I needed to learn how to control my own time and set boundaries. It took some work, but I have achieved great success. Do all of the other issues stemming from the black factor bother me? Of course they do, but as a business owner, I have learned that I have absolute power over most of it. I can choose what allows me to get angry. I can choose how I react in most situations.

One thing that helps me tremendously is my relationship with God. Dealing with some demons requires a supernatural solution. Yes, I said demons. My belief system leads me to believe that behind every malicious intention is a spiritual force. The source comes from either God or something that is not of God. Now before you gasp and toss this book into the "I'll finish it later pile", let me just say that this is my own personal experience that I am sharing with you. I totally understand that everyone may not share my same belief system and that people are in different stages of their own journey. What I hope that you take from my shared experience is that you need to lean into what works for you.

When you allow your triggers to push you to the point of losing self-control, you lose. Your business loses. Your brand loses. This is why it is critically important for you to self-reflect. Be honest with yourself. If you feel that your emotions will always get the best of you, then you need to put a system in place that removes you and your emotions from the situation. Lean into your staff for support. Hire and train employees that can make up for your deficiency. A good business owner knows his or her weaknesses and is modest enough to depend on their personnel to deal with issues that may be challenging for them to handle themselves.

Of course this is a great strategy if you have the staff to lean on. But what about if you are the only one running the show? What if you are the sole proprietor with no other employees to rely on?

You still have options. Unfortunately, the most obvious option is for you to brush up on your people skills and address your own demons. This will take time, but while you are waiting for your healing to begin, you should start thinking about an internal system that you can rely on to help you through certain customer service situations. By systems, I am referring to policies that you incorporate into your daily operations. These policies should govern the way you respond to customer service issues. The single most important aspect of these policies is that they should be visible to your customers. This could be on your website, in your contracts, or even a piece of marketing material if necessary. Well-established policies help you establish and enforce boundaries for your business, even if you are the sole employee. As stated previously, established policies will help you separate personal emotion from professional business affairs.

CHAPTER 26

Avoiding That Four Letter Word

A soft answer turneth away wrath: but grievous words stir up anger.
The tongue of the wise useth knowledge aright: but the mouth of fools
poureth out foolishness.

—Proverbs 15:1-2

Since I was a child, my mother taught me an important lesson that has stayed with me throughout my adult life. That simple lesson was "it's not what you say, but it's how you say it." I would happily argue that for the most part, this ideology is true at least 95% of the time. The other 5% has everything to do with what you say, and of course that 5% carries a lot of weight!

In certain customer service situations, what you say becomes very important. Of course, coming from an African American culture myself, we often make the correlation of "keeping it real" with disrespectfully saying anything we want to anyone we want, any time that we want. Yes, I said it. It may hurt some hearing it, but this is the most damaging mentality one can associate with sound business acumen. When running a business, one must be temperate in their word choice. Words have power. Words can inspire a positive or a negative environment.

As a black business owner, you need to critically understand how your use of words can affect your customers. Oftentimes, the agitation comes from the connotation of a particular word and the embarrassment that comes with its implications. It is your responsibility to have healthy awareness of that infamous four-letter word that may potentially upset your customers.

The word "can't" is often subliminally transferred to won't. In the customer's eyes you should be in control of your own business and there is nothing that you can or can't do. After all, it's your business and you are simply choosing not to help them, at least that's how it feels to them. It's important to note that while there are negative implications associated with the word "can't", there are situations where it is appropriate and necessary to acknowledge limitations or boundaries.

To really understand the power of the word can't, you have to understand the properties associated with the word.

A Limiting Mindset

When someone uses "can't" frequently, it may indicate a mindset that focuses on limitations rather than possibilities. It can hinder personal growth, problem-solving, and innovation.

Lack of flexibility

Saying "can't" can suggest inflexibility and an unwillingness to consider alternatives or explore different approaches. It can lead to missed opportunities for finding solutions or accommodating customer needs.

Negative perception of your capability

When individuals consistently use "can't" to describe their abilities or skills, it can create a perception of incompetence or lack of confidence. It may discourage others from relying on or trusting their capabilities.

Stifling creativity and growth

The word "can't" can discourage creative thinking, innovation, and personal development. It discourages individuals from exploring new possibilities or pushing their boundaries. The last thing you want is to create a culture of "can't" amongst your employees and staff.

Now that we understand the negative effects behind the word "can't", let's focus on how we can neutralize the power of this pessimistic word and redirect the conversation to regain positive control over a challenging customer service situation.

Here are a few examples on how we can achieve success by changing "what" we say and avoid immediately making the word "can't" our default response.

Level Up Exercise

Let's assume your customer asks you for something very specific and usual. It's something that you normally wouldn't do, but it wouldn't necessarily hurt you if you did it for your customer this one time. It's up to you to make a choice. Will you and your team level up and provide excellent customer service, or will you default to your usual defeatist approach? At this point, the only reason you should even consider the latter is if you are unsure of your ability, but lucky for you, this chapter shares tools that will help you level up your customer service ability! Here we will give you some alternative phrases that can help you get around the word "can't".

Instead of resorting to *"We can't do this"*, consider the following verbiage.

"This is something that we have not tried before; however, we can explore other options that may be suitable."

"From my experience, some of our other customers requested the same thing, and later found out that it wasn't right for them. Instead they opted to (insert offer), would you like to try that?"

"We haven't had much success doing it that way. May I offer you (insert product) instead. We've noticed that our other customers were extremely satisfied once they tried this."

"I apologize, but this a little bit beyond the scope of what we can offer, but I can suggest this alternative that may work well."

"This may be a bit challenging to do it this way, but let me find a workaround that may also work for you."

"We have some limitations in this area, but we can recommend trying... (insert offer).

As you can see, there are many ways that you turn a hard conversation around without leaving the customer totally disappointed. At the end of the day, all your customer wants is to have their problems resolved. Even if you cannot fulfill their specific request, you should always be prepared to offer an alternative solution. Remember...solve more, sell more!

CHAPTER 27

Mea Culpa Mishaps

While it is imperative to have clear communication with your customers, I would be remiss if I didn't acknowledge the fact that there are actually some situations that you may need to exercise extreme caution when speaking. While we are obligated to take ownership of customer service issues that happen in our shop, we also need to be careful not to unknowingly or unwillingly accept blame or take responsibility for something that could potentially land us in legal jeopardy. As I stated before, it is always best practice to obtain legal counsel for your business. If you have the means, try and have a good attorney on retainer for those sticky situations.

You should know that there is a fine line between taking ownership of an issue and admitting fault to a potential liability. This is a conversation that you should have (or will have) with your legal counsel well before any incident happens. You need to be aware of specific language you should probably avoid. You also need to coach your employees and staff around what to say or not say in those situations. While your employees should be taking control of an unfavorable situation, they should be advised not to admit to any wrongdoing that could potentially expose you and your business to a lawsuit.

At a minimum, you should have a set of stringent procedures written and accessible to the key individuals that will at some point, be a part of crisis management. The last thing you want is someone winging it on behalf of your company in a potentially litigable situation. Saying the wrong thing to a patron, media outlet, or posting inappropriately on social media can be devastating. In this day and age, people love to record drama. If there is an opportunity to create a melodramatic piece of content that gains thousands of views in minutes, then people will jump at the moment to record a situation that paints themselves as the victim and you as a horrible business owner.

When things begin to go south, the only thing you can really do in this case is rely on your policies and procedures handbook and your pre-rehearsed scripts. Your attorney should be able to help guide you on phrases to avoid. The one thing that you should always do is listen to the customer attentively and empathize with their feelings without inadvertently admitting any fault that can put you in a legal jeopardy.

Here are five things that you should avoid saying, along with alternative statements that will help you better navigate the situation.

"It's our fault"

Once you say it, so may it be, especially if someone is recording you. Always try to focus on the issue and look for a solution without assigning blame. It will be difficult to try and backtrack your statements once you put it out there.

An alternative would sound something like this…

"We apologize for any inconvenience caused and are committed to resolving this matter."

"We were wrong"

Again, it is imperative that you avoid using language that implicates you as the "at fault" party. Stay neutral and objective while discussing the issue and focus bringing the situation to a quick and fair resolution.

An alternative would sound something like this…

"We apologize for any inconvenience caused and are committed to resolving this matter."

"This should have never happened"

Of course any customer service failure should never happen, but it does, and you shouldn't antagonize your customers with thoughtless rhetoric. Most customers are pretty forgiving if mistakes are made, but in order for them to do that, they need to feel that you are honestly going to do your best to correct the mistake and make them whole.

An alternative would sound something like this...

"We will investigate the matter thoroughly and take necessary steps to resolve any challenges."

"You have the right to upset, I would be upset too"

While being empathetic is the cornerstone of customer service, this is not the time to become a willful ally in a potential legal crusade against your own business. Of course you should still express a level of empathy, but you should take care to do it strategically.

An alternative would sound something like this...

"We value your satisfaction and will do everything we can to make it right."

"We are responsible for all damages"

While it may be true that some of your customer's issue may be your fault, it would be prudent for you not to accept total blame until you have totally assessed the situation and truly understand what role you played in causing the issue at hand. Avoid assuming full responsibility for any damages or losses. Not only are you inadvertently admitting fault, you may also be putting the cart before the horse. Sometimes, monetary compensation is not the only thing a customer will accept to make them whole.

An alternative would sound something like this…

"We understand your concerns and will work towards finding a fair and satisfactory resolution."

There is no way to escape making mistakes, and a good business owner will have no problem admitting when they've made a mistake as they quickly move to resolve an issue. However, you must pay attention to that fine line between admitting that you made a mistake, and admitting fault to a potential legal fiasco. When your company admits mistakes, it demonstrates your integrity. Honesty should always be a part of your brand.

CHAPTER 28

Turning Customers into Fans

According to reports from McKinsey and Company, approximately 30 percent of black consumers are categorized as trend-setters, indicating their significant influence and impact on consumer trends. This presents a real opportunity for business owners. If you can win these trend-setters as customers, they will reciprocate by recognizing and promoting your brand through their networks. This is the kind of opportunity that you want to capitalize on and repeat. By prioritizing good customer service and tailoring it to meet the specific needs of these treasured customers, you can effectively transform them into loyal fans.

So what is a fan? A fan is a person who is extremely enthusiastic about and devoted to some interest or activity. It's said to be a variation of the word fanatic, which also means marked by excessive enthusiasm and often intense uncritical devotion. It's been noted that the word fan was related to baseball enthusiasts. In any event, you want your customers to be enthusiastic about your brand. In order to do that, you must align your brand with their yearning desire to be satisfied in a way that is unparalleled.

For those businesses that are looking to turn their African American consumer base into fans, there are a few things that you must consider.

1. Communication
The one sure way to quickly lose all respect from your African American consumer base is failure to communicate. In fact, over communication

is never a bad idea. Truthful communication fosters transparency and transparency fosters trust. You especially want your influential customers to have an undeniable sense of confidence in your products, services, and more importantly, your brand.

2. Customer Engagement

Engaging with the African American community beyond transactions can deepen customer loyalty. Businesses can achieve this by demonstrating a sincere desire to satisfy their needs when no one else will. It's simple: They talk about their issues. You listen and respond with products and services that offer a solution. By aligning your business with initiatives that resonate with their unique needs, you demonstrate your commitment to inclusion.

3. Empathetic Customer Service

Empathetic customer experiences are crucial to winning the hearts of African American consumers. By taking the empathetic customer service approach, you demonstrate a desire to embrace them where they are in their struggle. By demonstrating a genuine interest in understanding and meeting the specific and unique needs of African American consumers, businesses can cultivate lasting relationships. Demonstrating the ability to understand and share their feelings creates a relatable and authentic experience that helps validate their existence in the American economy.

4. Personalization

If you remember a certain old television show who's opening theme song suggested that "you want to go where everybody knows your name", then you can appreciate the sentiment. African American consumers are people first. They want to feel acknowledged and recognized on a level that rises above the usual biases and stereotypes they are used to encountering. Take the time to truly know your customers. Learn their names. Take time to understand why they're buying what they are buying and make their transactions all about them.

5. Follow Through

You have to more than follow up…you absolutely must follow through. The difference between follow-up and follow-through lies in your timing and your level of action. Follow-up typically refers to the act of checking in or providing additional information after an initial interaction or transaction. It involves reaching out to ensure that any outstanding matters are addressed, questions are answered, or commitments are fulfilled. Follow-up is proactive and helps keep the momentum moving forward as the relationship builds.

On the other hand, follow-through refers to the completion or execution of tasks, promises, or commitments made during an initial interaction or transaction. It involves taking action and delivering on what was promised or agreed upon. Follow-through demonstrates reliability, consistency, and a commitment to fulfilling obligations or meeting expectations. This is another compelling way to help build brand loyalty by proving your ability to fulfill their need.

6. Incentivize

I'm sure that every one of you reading this book is enrolled in some kind of rewards or loyalty program at your favorite stores. Why is that? Because those businesses understand that consumers are looking to save money while feeling special at the same time. A good loyalty or rewards program encourages customers to purchase more of your products or services, while simultaneously increasing the chances of them becoming loyal to your brand. Loyal customers buy more and are often willing to pay more, which can help you increase conversions, boost your sales, and grow your business. Brand advocates are important because people love to share their experiences. Statistics have shown that almost 90% of people are more likely to trust a brand that's been recommended to them.

There are truly many more ways that you can help turn customers into loyal fans, but these few listed here should give you a solid foundation on where to start. Businesses that recognize the significance of good customer service and proactively tailor their process to meet the needs of African Americans will find themselves rewarded.

CHAPTER 29

Back to Basics for Home-Based Businesses

O kay, I know this has been a lot of information to unpack and process. I know that some of you may be thinking that this information is great for someone that has a business with a physical location. I know you may be thinking, how does this apply to me, I'm just starting out? If this is you then hang on to your bookmarks. This information is just as useful and valuable even if you are a start up, a sole proprietor, or even if your business only exists in a virtual, digital, or home based space. All of the information and tools presented in this book are scalable! If you master these principles on a small level, then you will undoubtedly perfect them as you grow your business.

Let's assume you don't have a brick and mortar storefront, and honestly, unless you are selling merchandise, most businesses will not initially fall into this category. The one thing you have to consider is that with any business, there is always a customer service component that will need to be addressed. Just because you may not physically see your customer, you cannot and should not adopt the "out of sight, out of mind" mentality. Even if your business is a web based business, the principles discussed in **Chapter 5: Look the Part. Live the Part** can be beneficial as you establish and grow your business.

For starters, unless it is your absolute goal to remain anonymous, having a professional picture of yourself on your website can be paramount. When I say a picture of yourself, I don't mean using a cropped picture of yourself from the last family cookout. Invest in quality professional photographs. Put thought into your attire. Should you wear business attire? Would a uniform be more appropriate? Do whatever makes sense for your business, but be sure that your decisions will be a good positive reflection of your brand and business.

Along with your photo, take time to write an enlightening biography about yourself. When people feel comfortable with you, the more likely they will do business with you. This is particularly important for black business owners. Unfortunately, as a black business owner, you will almost certainly have to shake the stigma of being shady. It's unfortunate, but it occurs because there are some black owned businesses that have put that negative energy out into the universe by conducting business in an unscrupulous or unprofessional manner. Not only have they damaged their own reputations, they have called into question just about any black owned business that displays any hint of obscurity.

There are many important points regarding the optics of business and branding that I have already covered in previous chapters. With a few tweaks, these same principles can easily be applied to your non-brick and mortar business. The overall focus remains the same. How your customer views your brand is the cornerstone of a successful customer service experience.

The good thing is that you can control a good part of that experience. Whether a customer is logging onto your website, or calling you on the phone, you have an opportunity to create a memorable and pleasurable customer experience. You have to be the one to own the experience. All of it. Your smile should be heard on the phone. People should feel comfortable looking and learning about you on your website. No matter how small your business is, you should always be thinking about your customer service process on a grand scale. At a minimum, you should have some kind of basic policies in place that govern your customer's experience. It doesn't have to be an elaborate set of protocols stuffed into a three-ring binder; however, they should be well thought out and well-articulated.

As you can see, you don't have to be a customer service guru in the beginning; however, on the most basic level you will need to learn how to conduct your business in the most professional manner possible. As a smaller home-based business, you actually have a big advantage…the power of personalization. Because you are operating on a smaller scale, you can really elevate your customer's service experience by making each experience unique to each individual customer. Here are a few tips that can help you master this.

Tip 1: Establish Clear Communication Channels

Even as a small business it is imperative that customers can easily reach you through various communication channels. This may include email, phone, and even social media platforms. As stated in Chapter 5, there are many ways to ensure that all of these communication channels are presented in a professional manner. Just remember that consistency, timeliness and transparency are very important.

Tip 2: Personalize Your Communications

One of the easiest things you can do is personalize your customer's interactions with you. By personalizing your customer communications, you make them feel special. When sending emails or other marketing communication, be sure to address them by name. Customize and tailor your correspondence to address your customer's individual needs and concerns. Not many big businesses are able to do this consistently. This can be your secret weapon within the marketplace. Believe it or not, some customers really enjoy a personalized customer service experience. Some will even pay a premium for it. Remember, your customers have a choice on where and how they spend their money. You definitely want to make an extra effort to roll out the red carpet and make them feel even more valued when doing business with you.

Tip 3: Save the Data…

Keep a record of customer data such as birthdays, purchase history, or any other relevant information that helps you to individualize each customer's experience. Send birthday emails Send thank you notes. Send scheduled follow up communications after a purchase. Send special offers. Leveraging customer data not only helps you deliver customer service, it also opens up cross sell opportunities.

Tip 4: Be a Know it All

As a small or home based business you need to absolutely convince your customers that they can put all of their trust in you. Keep in mind that they may feel as if they are taking a gamble with a smaller business or brand. You need to make them comfortable, which means that you should be an expert when speaking about the products and services that you offer.

Tip 5: Get Feedback Frequently

Even as a home based business, you should be diligently gathering customer feedback via surveys, reviews, or direct communication. Use this information to identify areas for improvement. Keep in mind that most consumers might not let you know when you make a mistake. Outside of slamming you in an online review, they simply will not do business with you again. The simple gesture of allowing your customers to offer their feedback, shows a commitment to good customer service on your part. Don't be afraid to reach out to customers directly to discuss and rectify any issues.

Remember, delivering exceptional customer service is about more than resolving customer issues. but also about creating positive and memorable interactions. Building strong relationships with your customers can lead to repeat business, positive word-of-mouth, and increased customer loyalty for your home-based business.

Keep in mind that providing outstanding customer service goes beyond simply resolving customer issues. It's more about fostering positive and memorable interactions with your customers. Cultivating strong relationships with your customer base increases your potential to generate repeat business, circulate positive word-of-mouth reviews, and build customer loyalty for your home-based business.

CHAPTER 30

Customer Service Matters Online Too!

In today's environment, online businesses remain and will continue to remain a prevalent part of the sales ecosystem. However, do not think for one minute that you are let off the hook when it comes to providing an exceptional customer service experience online. As customers increasingly turn to online platforms for their purchasing decisions and support needs, business owners must begin to think about how they can deliver the same level of service that their customers would receive in a brick-and-mortar location. The pandemic has also immensely contributed to the rise in online sales. Online accessibility offers an unprecedented level of convenience. Consumers can buy anything, at any time, from anywhere, eliminating the finite constraints of physical locations and business hours. Online accessibility enhances the overall customer experience by putting the customer in the driver's seat and giving them a certain level of control.

Having an online presence should not be considered optional anymore. It's the new way of the world so you have to be prepared to make the choice to embrace it, or be prepared to be left behind. Giving your customer infinite access to your products and services means that you have the opportunity to exponentially increase your sales and revenue. In addition to bolstering your bottom line, positive online experiences play an important role in building trust and promoting brand loyalty. Think about it. You now have the uncanny ability to put a 24-hour mobile store in all of your customer's pockets with almost little to no overhead. This is certainly a huge opportunity and you do not want to blunder it away with sloppy online customer service practices.

Another thing that you need to consider is the vastness of the online community. You have the ability to connect with consumers from all over the world. Unfortunately, this can be a good or bad thing. It can be great if you are doing things well, but it can be a nightmare if you get things wrong; however, if you plan and execute your online presence strategically, you can create an overall customer experience that your customers will love and appreciate.

The ability to engage with your customers on such a limitless level is something that should be revered as priceless. This platform gives you the ability to make money while you sleep, but while you're sleeping, your customers may have questions or they may run into a customer service issue while they are shopping online. No matter what the issue is, you need to make sure that their concerns are addressed when the issue arises, even if it's 3 a.m. in the morning. In order to be successful at doing so, you will need to have systems in place. This particular set of systems may function a bit differently than your physical location would, but the basic principles of customer service will still apply. The biggest difference in application is automation.

You have to approach the online world understanding that there will be certain limitations regarding personal interaction; however, the customer should not feel that they are receiving any less service. How do you do that? Well…do you remember at the beginning of this book that I mentioned how a well-designed website is one of the components of your brand looking the part? Here is where it becomes applicable. Your website or landing page is a representation of the personal interaction your customer would expect to receive if they were visiting your store in person. They should be treated with the same warm and inviting welcome.

You will also need to understand that African American consumers will look for representation within your brand. When they land on your website, they should see themselves within the imagery. They want to know that they can trust your brand to cater their specific cultural needs, and you cannot and should not take that for granted. Here are a few things to consider as you analyze your own website and overall online presence.

Brand Strength

I cannot stress the importance of brand enough. It's usually the first thing that consumers will see and respond to. If they feel they can trust your brand, then they will spend their money with confidence. Online branding encompasses the visual elements, tone of voice, and overall personality of a business. Consistent branding across a website and other online platforms establishes a recognizable identity and fosters a sense of trust. If your website looks shady, people will most likely shy away from doing business with you online. If your language is offensive or you just cannot find the right voice to connect the customer to your brand, you will find it difficult to convert.

Remember, you have to look the part...especially online. You will not necessarily get a second chance to win a customer's trust with that undeniable charm you're used to spreading around. The human inter-action that we often rely on to help foster relationships will be defunct. In fact, the only interaction a customer will have with your brand will be within the context of your website. Within the framework of your website, you need to be sure that you align your brand's promise with a commitment to excellent customer service. The strength of your brand should be leveraged to help prepare your customers for a great customer service experience online.

User Experience

User experience or (UX for short) refers to a user's journey when interacting with a product or service. In this case, the user would be your customer and their journey would be their experience and engagement while they are visiting your website. UX design is the process of creating products or services that focus on providing meaningful experiences for users. These experiences often revolve around branding, usability, and overall design.

When thinking of UX design, you should be considering the entire journey a user experiences when interacting with your online brand. How is the user connected with your brand? What is their customer service experience like? Is it likely that they would return back to your website? Is it easy for them to access the information they need so that they can make a purchase?

A well-designed website makes it easier for customers to find the information they need and by providing straightforward navigation throughout the site, an intuitive layout, and by also having a responsive design making it easy for customers to access the information across different devices and platforms. Paying attention to your UX design will most certainly enhance the user's customer service experience by reducing frustration and making interactions smoother.

Customer Service Support
Websites will usually provide multiple channels for different levels of customer service support. These channels may include live chat, contact forms, FAQ pages, or even links to email their customer service department directly. These resources enable customers to have a means to access help at their fingertips. By seamlessly integrating these customer service tools into your business' website design, you give your customers an easy to navigate personal customer service experience. Having the ability to chat with a representative or send an email regarding a question about a service or product, is the same as if they were standing right in front of you or employees. The same rules of engagement apply. Instead of speaking, the customer is on the receiving end of what you are typing, so be mindful of your tone because you wouldn't want to inadvertently trigger your customer.

If you are offering these channels of service, make sure that they are available when you say they are available. There is nothing more frustrating than clicking on a chat button only to wait for minutes, only to realize that no one is there. The same pitfalls that can hurt your customer service reputation are the same pitfalls in the online arena, except they are digital. It'a also a good idea to make sure that your product and service knowledge databases are current and accurate. Customers will be leaning on the information presented on the website in lieu of a human customer service representative, so just like your employees need to provide correct and accurate information, so must your knowledge database.

Personalization

If you have not realized by now, technology is amazing. If you are paying attention and putting in the effort, you can maximize every online opportunity beyond your wildest imagination. Business owners can enhance customer satisfaction by personalizing service interactions. You should be able to leverage customer data and user preferences to capitalize on upsell and cross-sell opportunities. For African American consumers, this presents a very valuable and unique opportunity. This is the time to nurture those valuable relationships by demonstrating your ability to provide products and services that are important to them not only from a customer service point of view, but from a cultural point of view. African American consumers are not used to mainstream America "getting them;" that's why it is up to you to fill that void.

You should be looking to deliver those personalized experiences and improve their overall customer experience by offering other products and services that complement their sales habits.

Online Feedback

Processing customer feedback can be heartbreaking at times. Usually, it's a one-off customer service kerfuffle that somehow spiraled into a one-star negative review nightmare. Even one bad review can be devastating, but you should take special care to embrace those reviews, especially from your African American customers. Again, they are telling you what they want, so make sure that you listen. Giving your customers the ability to rate and review your service is one of the most significant things you can do. You give your customers a voice. You give them a degree of power that they necessarily may not get elsewhere. This type of engagement fosters a positive perception of your brand or business' commitment to customer satisfaction, and will inspire them to become loyal fans. By integrating these inclusive customer service practices online, you will strengthen the relationship with your African American consumer base.

Customer service is customer service, whether in person or online. The basic principles are the same. If something isn't working, fix it. One of the things about customer service online is that you are in complete control. You are really the sole force that drives your customer service engine. Your customer's online experience will truly be reliant upon how you design your online system to be. If it doesn't work, it's your fault. You won't have bad employee behaviors to blame.

CHAPTER 31

Internal Customer Service

In any organization, the significance of exceptional customer service is widely acknowledged. However, there is one aspect that often goes overlooked—internal customer service. Internal customer service refers to the interactions and support provided among colleagues within an organization. Just as external customers are vital to business success, so are internal customers—the employees. This chapter will delve into the importance of internal customer service, exploring how it fosters collaboration, enhances employee engagement, and ultimately contributes to the overall success of an organization.

Internal customer service plays a pivotal role in creating a collaborative culture within an organization. When employees prioritize serving each other with respect and professionalism, they lay the foundation for strong working relationships. In turn, those good internal behaviors will translate into good behaviors for your customers.

The impact of internal customer service on employee engagement cannot be stressed enough. When employees feel valued and supported by their own co-workers and team members, their overall attitude improves job satisfaction. Positive internal interactions create a sense of belonging and promote a more inclusive work environment. As a result, employees become more engaged, which directly translates into higher productivity, improved performance, and reduced turnover rates.

Internal customer service also promotes a sense of ownership among employees. This shared responsibility creates a strong sense of team spirit.

Internal customer service may often be overlooked, but its importance cannot be understated. By fostering collaboration, enhancing employee engagement, and contributing to overall organizational success, exceptional internal customer service creates a harmonious work environment where employees thrive and the organization flourishes.

CHAPTER 32

Pulling it All Together

"In everything, therefore, treat people the same way you want them to treat you, for this is the Law and the Prophets. (NASB).

—Matthew 7:12

The golden rule. It's simple, straightforward, and everlasting. I truly hope that you have enjoyed reading this book and I pray that I have been able to help you expand your perspective around the challenges that you may face as you strive to deliver exceptional customer service as a black business owner. Just to reiterate, when people say, "That's why I don't support black businesses", they are almost always talking about a poor customer service situation that they experienced. If black-owned businesses focus on providing exceptional customer service each time to counter "the black factor" that these companies are already up against, I wholeheartedly believe that we will hear that phrase "That's why I don't support black businesses" less and less.

Hopefully, we can collectively find common ground as we dismantle this all too familiar stigmatism that has black business owners feeling like pariahs in their own communities. There is a lot to be learned by way of the business owner and the consumer. I truly hope that my African American consumers find solace in the fact that this issue is being recognized and the behaviors that have left you feeling disappointed with black-owned business owners will hopefully be rehabilitated as business owners learn to embrace and apply some of the basic principles expressed in this book.

May I Help You? was designed to act like a well needed medication—bitter at first, but over time makes you better. I wrote this book with the intention of helping black business owners understand why and how they need to make customer service a priority. For African American consumers, customer service and solidarity go hand in hand. African American consumers need black-owned businesses and black-owned businesses need African American consumers. There is only one unifying principle between the African American consumer and the black-owned business. Respect. Respect for each other's time. Respect for each other's struggle. Respect for each other's perseverance to survive in a world that may not necessarily want to see us win.

While this book is dedicated and directed towards black business owners to assist them in becoming better stewards over their customers, there are many general principles that are not exclusive to black-owned businesses. Anyone looking to enhance their customer service experience are more than welcome to utilize the information and the tools provided in this book. Will this book solve every problem? Of course not. Nothing is absolute. Society changes. People's needs change, the way consumers like to shop may change over time, but the concept of the golden rule will remain unwavering until the end of time.

On the flip side, I am hoping that African American consumers will also read this book with an understanding that there is a level of patience and understanding that comes with supporting black-owned businesses. It shouldn't be, but it is. Does that mean that you should accept subpar service? Absolutely not. It does, however, mean that there needs to be a willingness to pay a little bit more from time to time (within reason of course!). It does mean that you should be a little bit more forgiving if the business does not get it right the first time. Give them an opportunity to make it right.

To my black-owned businesses, this execution of grace given by your African American customers should in no way be taken for granted. You need to get it right. You cannot continually ask your African American customers for third and fourth chances. Unless there is a major overhaul to the economic social structures in this country, there will always be challenges. It is up to you to navigate through those challenges. You owe it to your customers. It will be difficult. It will not feel fair. But that doesn't matter. We are a resilient people. There will always be factors not in our control, factors designed to hinder our progress; however, if we focus on perfecting those things that we can control, we can achieve success in the form of economic freedom.

The passage of John 13:1-10 in the King James Version of the Bible portrays an instance where Jesus, as an act of humility and service, washes the feet of his disciples. This story emphasizes the importance of selfless service and putting others' needs above our own. Similarly, in the realm of customer service, the focus should be on meeting the needs and serving your customers with care and empathy. This passage should remind us that true customer service involves humility, kindness, and a willingness to serve others, aligning with the principles of love and self-lessness demonstrated by Jesus in the biblical account.

I hope that "May I Help You" will inspire black business owners to embrace the concept of putting people first. The minute it becomes more about profit and less about people, failure is imminent. I wish you good success in your journey and I pray that you find success and blessings as you strive to elevate your customer's experience!

Appendix A

Here are a few A.C.I.E. based questions that you can incorporate into your interview process. These interview questions are designed to gauge a candidate's customer service skills, problem-solving abilities, communication skills, adaptability, empathy, and professionalism. Feel free to tailor the questions based on the specific requirements of your customer service role and the values of your organization.

1. Describe a situation where you provided exceptional customer service. How did you handle it, and what was the outcome?
2. How do you define excellent customer service, and why is it important to you?
3. How do you handle difficult or irate customers? Can you provide an example of when you handled that type of customer?
4. How do you balance the needs of the customer with the policies and limitations of the company?
5. Describe a time when you had to go above and beyond to satisfy a customer's request. How did you handle it, and what was the result?
6. How do you handle a situation where a customer is dissatisfied with the product or service they received?
7. Give an example of a time when you had to handle multiple customer inquiries simultaneously. How did you manage the situation effectively?

8. How do you approach building rapport and establishing a connection with customers?

9. How do you handle customer feedback, both positive and negative?

10. Describe a time when you had to communicate complex information to a customer. How did you ensure they understood it?

11. How do you handle confidential or sensitive customer information?

12. Give an example of how you would handle a situation where a customer's request is beyond the scope of your authority.

13. How do you prioritize tasks and manage your time effectively when dealing with multiple customer inquiries?

14. How do you stay calm and composed in stressful customer service situations?

15. Describe a time when you had to work collaboratively with a team member to solve a customer's problem.

16. How do you adapt your communication style to meet the needs of different customers?

17. Give an example of a time when you had to deliver difficult or unwelcome news to a customer. How did you handle it?

18. How do you stay updated on product or service knowledge to better assist customers?

19. Describe a situation when you received feedback or criticism from a customer. How did you respond to it?

20. What steps did you take to ensure customer satisfaction and retention?

References

1. McKinsey & Company. (n.d.). Marketing to the Multifaceted Black Consumer. Retrieved from https://www.mckinsey.com/capabilities/growth-marketing-and-sales/our-insights/marketing-to-the-multifaceted-black-consumer

2. Business Wire. (2018, May 17). NewVoiceMedia Research Reveals Bad Customer Experiences Cost U.S. Businesses $75 Billion a Year. Retrieved from https://www.businesswire.com/news/home/20180517005043/en/NewVoiceMedia-Research-Reveals-Bad-Customer-Experiences-Cost-U.S.-Businesses-75-Billion-a-Year

3. Zendesk. (n.d.). Customer Service Statistics. Retrieved from https://www.zendesk.com/blog/customer-service-statistics/

www.ingramcontent.com/pod-product-compliance
Lightning Source LLC
Chambersburg PA
CBHW071557200326
41519CB00021BB/6788